YOU CAN
PROFIT
FROM
STRESS

Dr. Gary Collins

YOU CAN PROFIT FROM STRESS

VISION HOUSE PUBLISHERS
Santa Ana, California 92705

Copyright ©1977 by Vision House Publishers, Santa Ana, California 92705.

Library of Congress Catalog Card Number 77-78669
ISBN 0-88449-062-9

Printed in the United States of America.

ACKNOWLEDGMENTS

The author wishes to acknowledge the help of the following individuals and publishers, who contributed to the production of this book in a variety of ways:

—to Julie Collins, my wife, who supports, encourages, loves, and helps me in so many ways, and who made a number of helpful suggestions for the improvement of this manuscript;

—to Georgette Sattler, my secretary, who typed the manuscript (under the pressure of deadlines, ringing phones, and innumerable interruptions), corrected errors, and made a number of good suggestions;

—to Medvis Jackson, my graduate student assistant, who worked on the index;

—to George Outland, Tom Podraza, and John Wales, my neighbors, who made their house available and for several weeks tolerated my piles of books and notes so I could write in a quiet place, free from interruptions;

—to Jack Hanslik and Chris Hayward, my publishers, who along with the other people at Vision House have encouraged me in this and so many other writing projects;

—to Bethany Fellowship, who granted permission to publish excerpts from Larry Christenson's *The Christian Family*, copyright ©1970;

—to *Chicago Today*, who gave permission to publish excerpts from Dorothy Storck's "I. C. Survivors' Therapy: Let It All Come Out," November 30, 1972, issue;

—to David C. Cook Co., who gave permission to publish excerpts from Joseph Bayly's *The View From a Hearse: A Christian View of Death*, copyright ©1969;

—to E. R. Dutton Co., who gave permission to publish excerpts from Walter McQuade and Ann Aikman's *Stress: What It Is, What It Can Do to Your Health, How to Fight Back*, copyright © 1974;

—to *Guideposts*, who gave permission to publish excerpts

CONTENTS

To Tim Malyon
and others like him
who have learned to profit from stress,
to inspire others in the process,
and to bring praise to God
in the midst of personal crises.

Part One

UNDERSTANDING STRESS

First Steps in Coping

Chapter 1
THE MEANING OF STRESS

It was a hot July afternoon as the bright yellow school bus lumbered past the orange groves and cotton fields of Southern California. Twenty-six school children, ranging in age from 5 to 14, were coming home from the last day of summer school. When he noticed an apparently stalled truck in the road ahead, the bus driver—a kindly and well-liked man who had been on the job for over 25 years—stepped on the brake, slowed his vehicle, and prepared to pass.

Suddenly three young men darted into the roadway, their facial features distorted by nylon stocking masks. Waving guns, they ordered the bus to stop, jumped aboard, and drove to a lonely wooded area, where the terrified children and their driver were hustled into two white vans and driven off to an unknown destination.

Meanwhile, back in the small farm community of Chowchilla, parents began to wonder why their children were late in getting home. Assuming that the bus had broken down, the school superintendent sent someone out to check the route. When nothing was found, the police were called in. Three hours later the deserted bus was discovered, lodged in a ditch and partially hidden by brush and bamboo poles. Where were the children? What had happened? Concern in the little town turned to alarm, and within hours police had begun what was to be the most massive search in California history.

Even as the search began, the 27 captives were many miles from home. In the dead of night, eleven hours after their abduction, the two vans were backed into a quarry.

The children and their driver were shown a three-foot-wide hole in the ground and ordered to descend into the darkened entrance. Buried six feet underground was an old moving van which was dirty, hot, and stuffy. Ventilation came only from two narrow pipes which ascended up to the ground level through the roof, and suffocation soon became a real possibility. But the air was to grow even more stifling when the captives placed two steel plates over the entrance hole and sped off into the night. Twenty-six crying children were left buried underground with one desperate adult, whose only source of illumination was a flashlight.

For the next sixteen hours the bus driver and some of the older children struggled to get out. They stood on a pile of mattresses and pushed up repeatedly against the steel plates. Eventually the cover began to budge, and finally the captives squeezed out of their underground cell. At 7:30 in the evening, 24 hours after the empty bus had been found, a startled quarry watchman spotted the bedraggled group wandering toward him, all in their underwear. The kidnapping victims had been found, tired and hungry but alive and well.

At 4 A.M. the next morning, a big air-conditioned Greyhound bus with its police escort wheeled into Chowchilla carrying 27 weary passengers. They were greeted with cheers and tears by relieved parents, townspeople, and a small army of reporters.

The kidnapping of the Chowchilla school children and their driver had kept the nation's attention pinpointed on the little California community for several hours. In other parts of the country, and even around the world, parents, thinking of their own children, had been able to empathize with the anxiety and tension of the worried Chowchilla townspeople. During the ordeal, the whole community had been under stress—the captives as they were taken to parts unknown and left to struggle for their freedom, and the families as they waited through the long hours, fearful for the safety and welfare of their children.

Looking over his cotton field a few days later, the bus

driver talked about his reaction to the stress: "The kids did their crying on the bus," he mused, "but I did mine after I got home. I walked down to the corner of the field and it just hit me." In their homes, some of the children had nightmares, and many of the parents must have thought frequently of the panic, anxiety, and fear which they had felt during their long vigil. The people of Chowchilla had learned the meaning of stress.

WHAT IS STRESS?

Stress is something which everybody experiences but nobody can quite define.

Stress is a force which creates upset stomachs, gnawing fear, splitting headaches, intense grief, excessive drinking, and violent arguments. Stress dulls our memories, cripples our thinking, weakens our bodies, upsets our plans, stirs up our emotions, and reduces our efficiency.

But stress also motivates us to study, encourages us to keep going when life gets difficult, spurs us to action in the midst of crises, helps us to mature, and at times makes life exciting.

The word "stress" was first used in physics and engineering. It referred to the severe forces that might be put on a building or bridge. It is this kind of stress which sometimes causes buildings to collapse because of the weight of ice or the power of a violent wind. Later the term "stress" was taken over by medicine, physiology, economics, sociology, and other fields of science, but for most people the word has come to have a distinctly psychological meaning.

There have been many scholarly attempts to define psychological stress,[1] but one of the best and most down-to-earth definitions came several years ago from a biologist named Hans Selye. Stress, he said, is essentially the wear and tear of living.[2] Stress for one person may differ from that experienced by someone else, but every day each of us experiences physical and emotional wear and tear resulting from the pressures of life.

According to Selye,[3] stress is not simply nervous tension, nor is stress something to be avoided or something which is always unpleasant. Riding in a roller coaster, playing a game of tennis, or watching an emotional TV program can all be very stressful, but these are stresses which we seek out and even enjoy. When it motivates us to action, stress can be good, but when it puts our bodies under prolonged physical and emotional pressure, then the very things which might have been stimulating and fun become destructive and unpleasant instead.

THE PREVALENCE OF STRESS

During a recent visit to North America, the director of Britain's National Association for Mental Health was interviewed by a Chicago newspaper. "The whole of the Western world is under stress," this visitor stated. "Our mode of living produces continuous stress from the moment we are born. It hits everyone. There is no escaping it. . . . Stress affects the apparently happy, healthy people just as much as natural-born worriers. I am left in no doubt," the director concluded, "that stress is the fastest-growing disease in the Western world."

Some people might question whether stress is really a disease, and others might wonder if it really is growing as fast as this health expert believes, but hardly anyone would deny its widespread influence.

Stress is not confined to old people or to middle-aged businessmen. It affects people of all ages and at every stage of life. The very young child must learn to cope with life outside the womb. He or she encounters the stress of hunger, wet diapers, and stomachaches, which a baby is helpless to relieve. Later the child must learn to walk, get along with brothers, sisters, and parents, adjust to school and the pressure from peers, cope with the frustrations of

Little League, or adjust to new math, crabby teachers, and spelling tests.

In our society the teenage years become even more stressful. Testing out new ideas and values, adjusting to an adult-sized body, learning to get along with the opposite sex, facing peer pressures to take drugs or engage in crime, struggling for grades, learning to live with sexual impulses—these and a host of other pressures can make adolescence a tumultuous period in life.

In college there may be loneliness, academic stress, the frustrations of learning for the first time to live away from home, and the problem of finding both a career and a mate. Marriage and parenthood bring new responsibilities, often accompanied by vocational pressures and the struggle to make ends meet financially. Then comes middle age, with the menopause and sometimes with a mid-life crisis, in which men and women face the fact that they are growing old and they probably will never succeed as they had always hoped. Insecurity, discouragement, alcoholism, and marriage breakup often follow and characterize this time of life.

Following this is retirement. It may have been anticipated with enthusiasm, but after the banquets and going-away parties the days can be long and dreary. Loneliness and financial pressures in the aged can be great, and they are often intensified by the despair of failing health and advancing years.

All of this sounds like a bleak picture. Happily, life isn't miserable for everyone, but all of us must face the stresses of growing older with the added pressures of deaths in the family, serious illnesses, divorces, or other crises.

TYPES OF STRESS

Whenever stress comes into our lives, it puts pressure on our bodies to adjust or adapt. Some people seem able to make this adaption quickly and efficiently, while others—

for reasons which we don't completely understand—are more easily overwhelmed.

To some extent, the way we react to stress depends on the nature of the stresses that we experience. Many stresses are *intense* but not long-lasting. Having an accident or operation, witnessing a tragedy, or being frightened—these stresses are usually unexpected. They can hit us with great force and very often they leave us in a state of confusion. Sometimes they cut us off temporarily from other people, so that we are lonely and overwhelmed by the circumstances. We may feel powerless to cope with the sudden change, and this sometimes creates panic.[4]

Prolonged stress, on the other hand, is less intense but lasts longer. Persisting loneliness, the slow falling apart of a marriage, the existence of a disease which doesn't get better, the pressure of war or of persisting financial problems, the unsuccessful struggle to reach a goal or fulfill some ambition—these are stresses which slowly wear us down, so that we become tired, irritable, and often physically ill.

Even minor stresses can at times be very disrupting. A ringing telephone or a crying baby may not in themselves be stressful for a young mother, but if both occur at the moment when dinner guests arrive, stress is greater because so many things are happening at once. Even one small stress can be a strain if it lasts too long. A loud stereo in the next apartment is simply annoying during the day, but the stress builds up if the music plays until four o'clock in the morning!

From these examples it might be easy to conclude that stress is an "American disease"—to use one writer's words—or that it is something of recent origin. Both of these conclusions appear to be wrong. There may be a few places in the world where stress is almost nonexistent,[5] but these places are difficult to find.

Recently, on a speaking trip which took me around the world, I discovered that stress was very common wherever I went. The people in Prague, Geneva, Madras, Tokyo,

Caracas, or Singapore may experience stresses different from those in Toronto, Chicago, or Kansas City, but stress is not limited to one part of the world. It is a worldwide problem.

Stress is also something very old. The increasing pace of modern society may be putting us under more intense stress than our ancestors faced, but for centuries men, women, and children have been forced to cope with stressful circumstances. Since the dawn of civilization humans have struggled for food, cowered before the elements, feared war, and faced the threat of plagues or disease. Many of the people we read about in the Bible encountered stress: Moses and thousands of Israelites, hotly pursued by Pharaoh's armies as they fled from Egypt; Jonah, cruising around the Mediterranean in the pitch-black belly of a huge fish; Nehemiah and his men, building the Jerusalem walls by hand while faced with the prospect of imminent attack; Paul the apostle, shipwrecked, beaten, and imprisoned; John the disciple, banished in loneliness to the solitary Isle of Patmos; Jesus as He faced trial and death, forsaken at the last minute by cowardly friends.

Then there was Job—one of the most dramatic historical examples of stress. In the early part of his life Job was a wealthy man. He was religious and morally upright, the father of a large family, famous and widely respected (Job 1:1-3). From what we can assume, he was also in good health.

Then things began to go wrong. First Job lost his possessions, and then his children. Next he lost his health and his prestige, ending up in such a deplorable, stressful state that for days his friends did nothing but sit in silence, staring at him.

Job's stresses came many years ago, but they are not much different from what we face today. Job had *financial* stress. This man who had been extremely wealthy suddenly became poor. His servants and possessions were wiped out, apparently in the course of a few minutes (Job 1:13-17). Like so many people today, Job found himself in economic difficulties, struggling with how he could make ends meet.

Then came *family stress*. Job's children were all together in a house which collapsed in a storm, killing all seven sons and three daughters (Job 1:18, 19). The devoted father whose custom it was to rise up early in the morning to pray for his children must surely have been plunged into intense grief. The only relative left was Job's wife. She could have been a real support and comfort to her husband in his time of greatest stress, but instead she criticized him, leaving the clear impression that there were serious problems within Job's marriage.

Status stresses also came into Job's life. He had been very successful in his life, but after his losses he must have felt like a failure, with everything gone and nothing to show for all of his labors. Finally, Job had *health stress*. Painful boils covered his entire body, and he looked so awful that he wasn't even recognized by his friends.

STRESS TODAY

Here in Job's life were the very things which create stress in most people's lives today: not enough money, problems in our marriages and families, grief, difficulties at work and with our struggles to be successful, and the failure of our health. Unlike the people of Chowchilla, most of us have never been kidnapped or faced with the sudden disappearance of our children. But we have other stresses— stresses which can affect our minds, wear down our bodies and hinder our getting along with other people.

Within recent years, many people have become deeply concerned about the extent and influence of stress in our society. "Stress is the virus of our era," a member of the West German parliament suggested recently. It has such an influence in stimulating disease that some have called it our number one health problem. According to a recent writer, our greatest medical need today is not new medicines or operative procedures—our greatest need is the discovery of new ways to cope with the inevitable changes and pressures in our personal lives.[6] That is what this book is about.

Solutions to the problem of stress can come from medicine, psychology, and other fields of science, but they cannot come from these alone. The solutions must also come from religion; people under stress need to see *purpose in life*. They need to know how the ancient teachings of religion can help them to relax and cope with life today. In a recent scientific book, the authors made a thought-provoking statement about stress and religion:

> The phenomenon of religious belief is a large subject, but . . . it must be said that religion in a devout believer has little equal as an allayer of stress. This is true of all religions, but particularly true of some. The Judaic-Christian tradition, for instance, takes on all the primal stresses, and if it does not dispose of them completely it makes them surprisingly bearable. Whatever role the believer plays in his world, however humble it [religion] argues, it is an important role, created by God for a reason. It tells him he can't win them all, and that the people who seem to win them all don't really win. Winners are often losers in the end, because winning isn't what matters anyway but meaning, truth, and love—and in the case of Christianity, life everlasting. And it tells him that God loves him and will go on taking care of him no matter what he does. Religion condemns sin, but in the very act of condemning makes a place for it. Unlike some systems of ethics, which seem cold and narrow by comparison, most religious creeds expect the individual to sin; they accept, however sorrowfully, his need to express rage, envy, covetousness, as well as repentance afterwards—and these are all things that people need badly to express.
>
> The waning power of religion is one reason why life has become so stressful in the Western world, and also why many people today are reconsidering and turning once again to religious faith, the more evangelical, it seems, the more popular.[7]

Before we can deal with the problems of stress, however, it is important that we understand what stress does to us and where it originates. These are the issues to which we turn in the next two chapters.

Chapter 2
THE EFFECTS OF STRESS

It happens every Thursday morning. I leave home about a quarter to eight and drive to the local Holiday Inn, where I meet for breakfast with a friend who works in a nearby counseling clinic. Usually we talk about our respective jobs or the latest trends in counseling, and then we leave in time to reach our offices by 9 A.M.

One morning a couple of years ago, my friend reported that on the previous night a fire had burned his clinic to the ground. In the weeks that followed, we talked about the plans to rebuild, and I shared his enthusiasm as he described the newer and larger facilities that would soon be available. When the building was completed, a dedication date was set, but two days before the official opening there was another fire. The investigators said it was arson, and the clinic staff wondered if the fire had been set by one of the patients who had suddenly disappeared. Once again the rebuilding process began, but the staff noticed some interesting changes in their behavior. At first there was excitement—a spirit of adventure as they talked to the fire marshal, were interviewed by the reporters, and readapted to the temporary offices set up in rented trailers. There was a feeling of unity, a drawing close to each other as they endured the disruptions together.

Before long, however, they began to get annoyed—at the inconveniences, the lost possessions, and the slowness of the insurance company. They even got irritable with each other and found themselves unconsciously taking out some of their feelings on the patients.

Then they became suspicious. They felt uncomfortable

about the fact that the arsonist had not been found. They began to wonder if one of the staff had set the fire, and each employee sensed the uncomfortable feeling that "even though I'm innocent, what if some of my fellow workers begin to suspect me." Nobody wanted to be last in leaving the building at night, and there was a tendency to avoid walking alone to the parking lot. Whereas the counselors had previously decorated their offices with pictures and plants, no one wanted to do this any more. "I can counsel just as well between four bare walls," somebody joked.

This joking persisted for a few days—an uncomfortable humor which let people express their tension but which was too threatening and close to reality for it to be really funny.

Suddenly it was all over. After a couple of weeks there was no further talk about the fire and no joking. It appeared that the staff just wanted to forget about the whole thing and get on with the task of doing their jobs and rebuilding their facilities.

THE PHYSICAL EFFECTS OF STRESS

The reactions of these people following the fire illustrate that it is not possible to experience stress of any kind without its affecting us in some way. Even the mildest change in our lives—like going on a vacation or winning a prize—adds to our total stress and can have an adverse effect on our bodies or psychological stability.

Consider what happens to animals when they are frightened or in other ways put under stress. Usually they either run or attack. When they "freeze" in one spot, this is only temporary. Let the stress continue or get worse and the animal eventually will run off or attack. This has been called "the flight-or-fight reaction," and it is not limited to animals. When the stress is great, human beings also have a desire to get out of the way or to fight off the pressure as best they can.

This running or fighting puts an added strain on the body. Because of the effort involved, we must be mobilized physically for the extra action, and this is precisely what happens, *automatically*. Whenever stress comes along, more sugar flows into the blood to give us energy, our senses become more alert, our muscles get tense, we breathe faster, our hearts beat more rapidly, and our whole bodies get geared up. This can be useful when we are in real danger—on a freeway, for example, or facing a sudden crisis which demands all of our skill and alertness.

But what if the stress is more subtle? What if it comes from noisy kids or struggling with a tense home situation? At these times the body still gets aroused physically, but it is inappropriate for us to react by flight or fight. We must control our emotions and clamp down on our reactions. The body therefore begins to fight against itself. It is aroused for action, but the action is squelched. Naturally, our systems can't take this for long. As a result there may be inner tension, physical disease, or mental breakdown. The body's automatic reaction, which once was a lifesaver for hunters and warriors, has in our age become a crippler and sometimes even a killer.

Stress and Ulcers

Consider, for example, the problem of ulcers. Everybody knows that business executives are supposed to get ulcers, and sometimes men even joke about this being a badge of masculinity or an indication that they have finally reached the pinnacle of success in life. It would be more accurate, however, to say that ulcers are a mark of worry, tension, and the inability to control our stresses.

Several years ago some New York doctors were called to treat a man named Tom, who had severely damaged his esophagus by drinking hot clam chowder.[1] Since Tom could no longer swallow, the doctors pulled a portion of his stomach lining through the abdomen. This made it possible for Tom to feed himself by putting food directly into his stomach. Nothing tasted very good, but Tom was kept alive and the researchers were able to see how his emotions affected his digestion.

When Tom got angry or resentful, the lining of his stomach would swell and there would be an increase in the appearance of hydrochloric acid. This was especially true when Tom couldn't do anything about his stress. In 1946, for example, there was a coal shortage which Tom blamed on the politicians (whom he called "a bunch of crooks") and on a dealer who had promised to supply coal but hadn't done so. Tom was resentful but powerless to do anything about the problem. Soon his stomach became very red and began to bleed. The extra amounts of digestive acids began to gnaw at the stomach lining, and Tom found that he was a prime candidate for ulcers.

Today it is estimated that eight to ten million Americans suffer from ulcers. Often (although not always) these are highly competitive, go-getter men, women, and children.[2] They feel pressure from the world around them, but there is a lot of inner pressure as well—an inner drive to succeed and to get ahead.[3] Whenever they accomplish a particular goal, they set their aspirations higher and continue pushing. This keeps the body under such a constant state of physical alertness that the stomach lining begins to bleed and becomes irritated by the increased production of acids. And this is the start of an ulcer.

Studies with animals under stress have taught us something else. One of the biggest producers of ulcers is stress that you can't do anything about. We saw this with Tom, who felt frustrated but helpless in the face of a coal shortage. When a person under stress can't predict what will happen, or can't really do much to make things happen, he or she is a prime candidate for ulcers which are caused by the pressures of life.

Stress and the Heart

While it is well-established that stress can bring on ulcers, only recently have we begun to see a relationship between stress and the heart.

Heart attacks are largely a modern problem. Although

they have been reported in the medical literature for centuries, as recently as the late 1920's this disease was rare in North America. Then things began to change, until now in the United States over a million people have heart attacks every year. Most of the victims are men over the age of 65, but women have heart attacks too, and so do younger people (and the incidence of heart disease in these two groups is rising sharply).

What causes heart attacks? According to Dr. Michael DeBakey, the well-known heart surgeon, nobody knows for sure.[4] It is generally agreed that things like high blood pressure, a large amount of cholesterol in the blood, lack of exercise, obesity, and cigarette smoking all contribute to heart disease, but more and more it is beginning to appear that the single greatest cause of heart attack is the stress of life.

This is a view that has been held with special enthusiasm by two San Francisco cardiologists named Meyer Friedman and Ray Rosenman. These men divide the population into two broad categories, Type A and Type B.[5] The Type A person is ambitious, aggressive, self-demanding, competitive, and pushing to be successful. He or she "goes all the time" and is driven by the clock. In contrast, Type B people are more casual. They are less competitive, less worried about the time, and not so preoccupied with achievement. The two types even differ in their approach to relaxation. Type B can enjoy casual conversation and forget his work during a game of golf. Type A competes as intensively in sports as elsewhere and is even inclined to take up jogging. That, states Dr. Friedman, is the best way for such people to achieve sudden death at age 35.

While it probably is true that nobody fits these categories exactly, most of us tend to fall into one or the other of the two classifications.

After studying this problem for over twenty years, Drs. Friedman and Rosenman believe that when people live a Type A lifestyle there is seven times more risk of heart attack than with a Type B mode of living. Even if they don't smoke, get little exercise, show normal blood pressure, and have no family history of coronary disease, Type A people are more likely to have coronary attacks than Type B's.

Perhaps the influence of stress on the heart is even more clearly shown in the story of Roseto, Pennsylvania. Founded in the 1880's by Italian immigrants, the citizens for many years had lived in the United States with the same lifestyle as they had enjoyed in Italy. Theirs was a warm, congenial community with close family ties and a love of Italian food. Meals would go on for hours as the residents consumed massive quantities of spaghetti, pasta, and dishes rich in olive oil and lard—all washed down by wine. In spite of this high-cholesterol diet, when the Rosetans were studied in 1961 it was found that they suffered heart attacks at a rate of only one-third the normal average! The men and women of Roseta appeared to be in good health, and they lived to ripe old ages.

When the Rosetans were studied again in 1971 the researchers found radical changes. Roseto had become Americanized! The average income had gone up, television had replaced conversation, and many of the men had become executives who commuted to work as their children began going away to college. Cars on the street had become larger, stores had become more aggressive in selling their wares, and the long leisurely meals had ended. Now the Rosetans ate French fries and hamburgers—on the run. And what about the heart-attack rate? It had leaped to three times the national average! "Most of the men who had heart attacks," the research team concluded, "were living under stress and really had nowhere to turn to relieve that pressure."[6]

Disease and the Stress of Life

The past twenty years have given rise to a great number of research studies showing the influence of stress on the body. It has been demonstrated, for example, that stress can have an influence in accentuating or producing migraine headaches, arthritis, backaches, and high blood pressure. Other research shows that stress can create impotence, frigidity, premature ejaculation, and menstrual irregularities. Sometimes stress even stops menstruation entirely for awhile—a fact which can send wayward adolescent girls and their equally guilty boyfriends into sheer terror. Then there is the influence of stress on aging. People who live hard lives wear out faster, especially if the stress of life involves a string of failures.

Researchers in greater numbers are now turning their attention to the influence of stress on an even more mysterious disease—cancer. In a study of 450 adult cancer patients, psychologist Lawrence Leshan found three prominent characteristics of stress. Most of the patients had lost a close personal relationship immediately prior to the disease, about half of the patients had trouble expressing hostility, and about a third showed tension over the death of their parents.[7]

Can we conclude from this and similar research that *stress alone* causes cancer, heart attacks, or any of the other physical symptoms we have mentioned? Probably not. But we do know that _stress is a key influence in illness,_ and that those diseases not caused by stress alone may still be influenced by the pressures of life. Stress puts the body on the alert and makes it more susceptible to disease. This has been clearly shown in the fascinating research of a University of Washington physician named Thomas Holmes.[8]

What to Do with Your LCU's

In a study of over five thousand patients, Dr. Holmes and his associates had discovered that disease very often follows any event in life, whether good or bad, which requires us to adapt or to change our reactions in some way. This led Holmes to devise a test for measuring the influence of change. Several hundred people of different ages and from different countries were given a list of the events shown in Table 1 and were asked to indicate how difficult it

━━━ TABLE 1 ━━━
THE STRESS OF ADJUSTING TO CHANGE

RANK	EVENT	L C U POINTS
1	Death of spouse	100
2	Divorce	73
3	Marital separation	65
4	Jail term	63
5	Death of close family member	63
6	Personal injury or illness	53
7	Marriage	50
8	Fired at work	47
9	Marital reconciliation	45
10	Retirement	45
11	Change in health of family member	44
12	Pregnancy	40
13	Sex difficulties	39
14	Gain of new family member	39
15	Business readjustment	39
16	Change in financial state	38
17	Death of close friend	37
18	Change to different line of work	36
19	Change in number of arguments with spouse	35
20	Mortgage over $10,000	31
21	Foreclosure of mortgage or loan	30
22	Change in responsibilities at work	29
23	Son or daughter leaving home	29
24	Trouble with in-laws	29
25	Outstanding personal achievement	28
26	Wife begins or stops work	26
27	Begin or end school	26
28	Change in living conditions	25
29	Revision of personal habits	24
30	Trouble with boss	23
31	Change in work hours or conditions	20
32	Change in residence	20
33	Change in schools	20
34	Change in recreation	19
35	Change in church activities	19
36	Change in social activities	18
37	Mortgage or loan less than $10,000	17
38	Change in sleeping habits	16
39	Change in number of family get-togethers	15
40	Change in eating habits	15
41	Vacation	13
42	Christmas	12
43	Minor violations of the law	11

would be to adjust to each. The results showed remarkable agreement. People had similar opinions about how much effort was required if they were to cope with each of the events on the list. The researchers were then able to assign scores to the list of life events, scores which have been called "life change unit points" or LCU's.

Before you read any further, you might want to check all of the items in Table 1 that have applied to you during the past year. Add up the points to get your total LCU score. According to Holmes' research, if you scored less than 150, there is only once chance in three that you will have a serious change in your health during the next two years. If you scored between 150 and 300, your chances rise to about 50-50. If you scored over 300 points, be careful. There is an 80 percent chance for a major health change (disease, surgery, accident, mental illness, etc.) in the next two years.

Life change even has a bearing on accidents. In one experiment Holmes collected LCU scores from a group of college athletes at the beginning of a football season. When the season was over, 9 percent of those with scores less than 150 had had injuries, 25 percent of those in the 150-300 range had been injured, and 50 percent with scores of over 300 had had accidental injuries![9] Based on this and other studies, Holmes has concluded that life's changes can influence the existence of disease (whether it occurs), the time of disease (when it occurs), and the severity of disease (how bad it is).[10]

Recently I presented these figures in a classroom discussion, and a distraught student approached me after class. "What can I do?" he asked. "I have over 400 points." As we talked further I suggested that for the present he should, if possible, avoid any more of the events listed in the chart. In this way he could work at keeping his LCU total low. But I also had a word of encouragement for the student.

"Maybe you've already had your health change!" I said, while autographing the cast that had recently been placed on his ankle.

THE PSYCHOLOGICAL EFFECTS OF STRESS

The closest I have ever come to being killed was on the New Jersey Turnpike as we were traveling toward Philadelphia. I was riding in the back seat and suddenly became aware that the big truck on the left was moving into our lane. Clearly he didn't see us, and neither did the man in the truck on our right. The driver of our car sounded the horn, slammed on the brakes, and was able to avoid an accident by inches. I can only guess what this did to me *physically*, but I know what it did *psychologically*! I experienced an overwhelming sense of relief, along with a fear for our safety on the rest of the trip. I should have known that my friend in the driver's seat was shaken even worse and wasn't likely to get close to any trucks in the immediate future!

Alarm

When stress like this comes into our lives we may react in a variety of ways, but, according to Hans Selye, the body always goes through three distinct stages.[11] Selye, who is currently the number one expert on stress in the world, found that stress always triggers first what he calls an *alarm reaction*. This is a mobilization of the body with all its resources. It is a "call to arms," an arousal of the body for action.

Sometimes we never get beyond the alarm reaction. If we are killed or seriously injured there is nothing more we can do. In some cases the alarm reaction sends us into a state of shock and causes us to "freeze"—like a scared rabbit. This has been the experience of many pilots when they realize that their planes are crashing. They wait until the last minute before bailing out, and at times they don't jump soon enough. "I saw the truth but I did not want to accept it," said one pilot who did survive. "I could not reconcile myself to the obvious fact that we were going down. I thought there might still be a chance to pull back up."

Resistance

According to Selye, we can't stay in the alarm reaction stage very long. It's too draining on the body. Eventually we have to take some kind of reaction, and this occurs during the *stage of resistance*. Here we begin to fight the stress—physically, psychologically, and in any other way possible. We may remove ourselves from the stress situation, try not to think about it, attempt to change it, or grit our teeth and determine to survive it. If we are able to cope with the stress successfully we return to normal again, but if the stress persists, eventually we begin to buckle under the strain.

Collapse

This leads to the *stage of exhaustion*, in which we collapse under the pressure. Many people in mental hospitals have arrived there because of an inability to keep on resisting stress. Psychologically and perhaps physically they have given up the struggle.

Chicago newspapers recently carried the story of a 33-year-old man who went on a rampage at work one day, killing three executives of his company, injuring two co-workers, and then shooting himself. Everybody who knew this man was astonished. He was popular at work, a good neighbor, and someone who got along well with his family.

But the man lived under almost constant pressure. The company where he had worked for several years was known to be part of a high-pressure, intensely competitive business. To protect the firm against theft of its designs and production plans, there were closed circuit TV cameras, burglar alarms, iron gates, and a variety of other security devices. Employees were told never to discuss their work after hours, and apparently for this one man the pressure was too great. For as long as possible he resisted the stress and tried to cope with it. Eventually he could resist no longer and collapsed in an irrational outburst that left four people dead in a hail of bullets—including himself.

There are very few people, of course, who handle stress by going berserk, but the work of Selye and others has shown us that stress can influence us in predictable ways. It very often spurs us to action and can result in greater effort, more efficiency, increased productivity, better discipline, and even spiritual growth. But stress also takes a toll, especially if it is prolonged. It can make us irritable, hard to get along with, tired, anxious, apathetic, and angry. If it persists it can lead to truancy, alcoholism, and psychiatric disorders. Stress is a costly virus which can harm us physically and psychologically. It can also influence us spiritually.

THE SPIRITUAL EFFECTS OF STRESS

After his conversion, the Apostle Paul had a difficult life. In his Second Letter to the Corinthians he describes some of the stresses he encountered:

> Five times I received from the Jews thirty-nine lashes.
> Three times I was beaten with rods, once I was stoned, three times I was shipwrecked, a night and a day I have spent in the deep.
> I have been on frequent journeys, in dangers from rivers, dangers from robbers, dangers from my countrymen, dangers from the Gentiles, dangers in the city, dangers in the wilderness, dangers on the sea, dangers among false brethren;
> I have been in labor and hardship, through many sleepless nights in hunger and thirst, often without food, in cold and exposure.
> Apart from such external things, there is the daily pressure upon me of concern for all the churches . . .
> (2 Corinthians 11:24-28.)

In addition to all of this, Paul had a "thorn in the flesh." Three times he asked God to take it away, but when it persisted the Apostle concluded that it was keeping him humble and enabling him to grow spiritually (2 Corinthians 12:7-10). From these and other verses in the Bible we get the impression that Paul tried to see the positive side of his stresses and used them as growing experiences.

> We are pressed on every side by troubles, but not crushed and broken. We are perplexed because we don't know why things happen as they do, but we don't give up and quit. We are hunted down, but God never abandons us. We get knocked down, but we get up again and keep going. These bodies of ours are constantly facing death, just as Jesus did; so it is clear to all that it is only the living Christ within us who keeps us safe.
>
> Yes, we live under constant danger to our lives because we serve the Lord, but this gives us constant opportunities to show forth the power of Jesus Christ within our dying bodies. Because of our preaching we face death, but it has resulted in eternal life for you (2 Corinthians 4:8-12 TLB).

Paul knew that he could overcome his stresses, but he also realized that stress could cause people to go down spiritually. It had caused John Mark to give up the ministry. Demas forsook the faith because of a love for the world, and even Paul himself seemed to be struggling with the stress of loneliness in the last letter he wrote to Timothy (2 Timothy 4:9-21).

Most of us discover that stress can have one of two influences on our relationship with God: it can draw us closer, or it can cause us to turn away in bitterness and disappointment. For some of us we even vacillate, alternating between prayer and an angry, frustrated rejection of spiritual things.

There is no doubt that stress has a profound influence on our physical, psychological, and spiritual lives. Stress can motivate us to action and growth, but it can also harm and even destroy us.

What then can we do about this malady of our age? The first step to real mastery over stress is to discover what causes it. Where does stress begin and how does it get such a strangling grip on our lives? The next chapter tries to answer these questions.

Chapter 3
THE ORIGINS OF STRESS

What do you think is the most stressful occupation in the world? Contrary to what you might think, it's not being a mother or trying to handle a house full of teenagers. It's not being a business executive, physician, Marine recruit, or politician, stressful as these occupations may be. According to recent reports the most stressful job in the world is that of air traffic controllers. These are the people who use radar to guide airplanes in and out of airports and who are responsible to prevent collisions in the sky.

According to Dr. Richard Grayson, president of the American Academy of Air Traffic Control Medicine, there are an estimated 2500 to 7500 near misses in the skies over America each year. The air traffic controllers live under constant pressure that they will make a mistake—a mistake which could cause hundreds of deaths. According to Dr. Grayson, "a narrowly averted midair collision caused by one of these conscientious, intelligent, punctilious young men has the same effect on him as if he himself had just escaped death by a hair's breadth."

Shortly after a near miss, one of the controllers described his feelings this way: "I felt like I had just been in a bad automobile accident and had come out of it unscathed. I was nauseated, felt weak. My heart was racing and my hands were sweating." Such pressure has given the controllers the highest ulcer rate of any vocation. One third of these people have peptic ulcers (compared to a rate of one in ten for doctors and lawyers), and in the opinion of Dr. Grayson another third are on their way to developing them.[1]

It is not difficult to understand why air traffic controllers feel the pressures of their job so keenly. Theirs is work which carries weighty responsibilities, demands constant vigilance, and involves the frustration of working with radar and communication equipment which they consider outdated. Little wonder that these people are anxious, irritable at home, and sometimes unable to sleep well or eat.

STRESS OR FUN?

But what about the rest of us? What causes stress in our lives? This is difficult to answer. In the first place, the list of situations which cause stress can be almost endless: monotony, lack of time, being crowded too closely with others, isolation, lack of changing stimulation, noise, confrontation, competition, distractions, failure, pollution, lack of privacy, pain, change, and illness, to name a few.

Second, it is difficult to identify the causes of stress because almost anything that one person finds stressful somebody else finds enjoyable. Take roller coasters, for example. One of my daughters loves them, my wife doesn't even like to look at them, and I tolerate them only in the interest of trying to be a good father!

Noise is another example. While groups of citizens form committees to combat rising decibel levels in the community, their children happily turn the stereo to a level which, to say the least, is deafening—some would say maddening!

Recently two psychologists, experts on urban stress, gave an even more fascinating example.[2] For many years, they noted, a common way of studying stress in the laboratory was to have a person plunge his hands or feet into a bucket of ice water. In New York, however, members of the Polar Bear Club jump into the frigid Atlantic every January and everyone claims to enjoy the swim—at least until they get pneumonia!

SOME GENERAL CONCLUSIONS

All of this leads to some general conclusions about the origins of stress. First, and most obvious, what is stressful depends on the individual person. Some things, like a tornado or terminal illness, would be stressful to everyone, but there are many other situations which bother some people greatly but do not affect others at all.

Second, circumstances have a major bearing on what is stressful. If a thief approached me from behind and grabbed me around the neck, this would be very traumatic. If my wife did the same thing in a surprise hug, I'd be delighted. When my lawn is getting mowed, the noise of the lawnmower does not disturb my work, but my reaction may be different if the noisy lawnmower is next door. It all depends on where and when something occurs.

Third, that which is predictable is less stressful. People who live near train tracks hardly even notice when the regular 3:52 A.M. train goes by, but the visitor usually awakes. If we know a stress is coming, and when it will arrive, we can tolerate it better. If we can't predict what is coming next, stress is more difficult to handle.

Finally, and perhaps most important, is the ability to control a situation. In one interesting research study, two groups of working people were bombarded with identical noise. One group could push a button to turn off the noise if it became too bothersome, but the other group had no button to push. In both groups the work got finished, and since few people had turned off the noise, both groups did their work in an equally noisy setting. But there were some startling differences. People who had the option of turning off the noise were less irritable, less inclined to make mistakes, and more willing to help one another. The noise hadn't bothered them because they knew they could control it.[3]

Researchers in Sweden once did a study of passengers who commuted to work by train.[4] To their surprise, it was found that the traveling was less stressful for people who got on the train first than for those who boarded later. Obviously the people who got on at the first stop could decide where to sit, where to put their packages, and who would sit next to them, whereas the passengers who boarded later didn't have this freedom to control their environment. The stress of traveling, therefore, was greater for those who came aboard later, even though they had a shorter ride. I feel the same about airplanes. I don't like "open seating," in which you pick a seat on your own. The trip is more enjoyable for me when I can get seat assignments in the airport before boarding the plane.

All of this can have great implications for, say, the mother of small children. The crying and misbehavior of young people is unpredictable and sometimes uncontrollable. If there is no escape, the stress can be overwhelming for the mother. Perhaps this is one reason why distraught parents so often beat their children or yell at them, even in public places.

FRUSTRATION

We turn now to some of the most common causes of modern-day stress, beginning with frustration. Frustration comes when our progress toward some desirable goal is blocked. The prospective medical student who gets a D in chemistry is frustrated, in this case because something outside him, in his environment, has blocked his advancement in a career. At other times frustration is internal. The would-be musician who has no musical talent or the short boy who wants to play basketball are frustrated because of inner limitations.

Life is filled with frustrations, and these can be very stressful. Sometimes we react by trying to find another way to reach our goals, or at times we might change our goals altogether. Near my home, for example, is a railroad crossing where (usually when I am in a hurry!) trains block the traffic. On occasion I have turned my car around and gone another way, which takes me under a bridge but lets me go around the obstacle. If I am really late, I can decide to give up altogether, changing my plans and going back home. More often, however, I sit angry and fuming. This, according to some well-established psychological research, is the most common reaction. Psychologists call it the "frustration-aggression hypothesis." Stated simply, it says that whenever people get frustrated they have a tendency to respond with aggression.

This aggression can be of two types. Sometimes we react *overtly*, lashing out with our tongues or maybe with our fists. This is like blowing our horn at the train. Such behavior isn't usually acceptable in polite society, so it is more common for us to react *passively*. Here we may smile and be charming on the outside while we seethe with anger inside and look for more subtle ways to express ourselves.

Smiling on the Outside, Seething on the Inside

There are many ways in which we can express anger subtly. Griping is one; gossiping is another. Sometimes we simply refuse to cooperate, or we may try goldbricking, which involves doing little or nothing while we pretend to carry out an assigned task. Another technique is what psychologists call scapegoating—directing our anger to some person or group other than the source of our troubles. Frustrated air traffic controllers who blow up at their wives may be expressing anger not at work (where they might risk getting fired for expressing anger), but at home, where things are safer. As everybody knows, such tactics are not limited to air controllers! Even little children slam the door when they are really mad at mother!

Then there is humor. As we will see in the next chapter, this can be a good way to handle stress, but it can also be destructive. When a man makes a sarcastic or joking comment about his wife in public I always wonder why. The wife is powerless to respond, at least then, lest she appear to be a poor sport who can't take a joke. But the joker may be revealing more about himself than he thinks. He is expressing his frustrations publicly, subtly, and in a way which makes another person feel put down and discredited.

Frustrations are part of the stress of living, but not all frustrations affect us in the same way. As you might expect, the stress is greater when we are stopped from reaching an *important* goal than when we are blocked in our progress to an *unimportant* goal. The stress from frustration is also reduced when we are given a reasonable explanation for the interference, and when the frustration did not come as a complete surprise.[5] Frustrations, however, force us to change our behavior in some way, and that brings us to a second origin of stress.

CHANGE

One of the most significant and oft-quoted books to appear in recent times was a meticulously researched volume titled *Future Shock*.[6] "In the three short decades between now and the twenty-first century," author Alvin Toffler began, "millions of ordinary, psychologically normal people will face an abrupt collision with the future." The book defined future shock as a "dizzying disorientation brought on by the premature arrival of the future" and went on to present fact after fact to support the idea that our society is changing at breakneck speed. This change, with its novelty and increased pace of living, is so rapid that most of us can't keep up.

Human beings are remarkably adaptable creatures. Some of us have tried to ignore cultural changes, sleepwalking our way through life as if nothing has altered since the 1930's and nothing ever will.[7] Others of us have learned to roll with the waves of change, hoping not to be tossed about too abruptly, but keeping up as best we can. We have learned to regularly change our hairstyles and lifestyles, to accept the new math and a new morality, to adjust to new ideas and perhaps a parade of new neighbors, and to recognize that no one person will ever be able to keep up-to-date on everything.

All of this change, however, puts us under incredible stress, and there are clearly limits to our adaptability. Because of its uncertainty and rapidity, change can easily get us confused or discouraged. The anxiety in our society, tenseness, fatigue, and widespread struggles to find meaning or an anchor for the future can all be attributed to our inability to cope forever with change. The index to Dr. Selye's most recent book does not mention change, but I suspect he would agree that many people today are in the stage of resistance, trying to cope. If we don't learn how to handle the changes of life, more and more of us will collapse into the stage of exhaustion. We simply cannot take the pressure forever.

Coping with Change

Selye has given one technique for coping with change. "Trying to remember too many things is certainly one of the major sources of psychological stress," he writes. "I make a conscious effort to forget immediately all that is unimportant and to jot down data of possible value."[8]

Toffler is more specific. We need to anticipate change, he suggests, by training specialists in "futurology," to find ways to cope with and plan for what is ahead. Six years after the appearance of his book, however, Toffler didn't seem to be very encouraged with our progress in this direction. We are still in a crisis, he said in an interview, and things aren't getting any better:

> The changes are simply tremendous—changes in technology, family structure, sexual values, raw material bases, ecology, you name it. All these systems are in upheaval, but there is no sense of direction, no sense of purpose and very little feeling that anybody is taking change into account in planning for the future. What is happening is obviously quite radical, at least on a scale with the Industrial Revolution; and I don't think we are going to make it through the next 20 or 30 years if we stay on our present course.[9]

Such pessimism about the future creates another stress for many people, and it points to the problem of fear.

FEAR

Let's assume that you are a psychologist interested in doing an in-depth study of psychological stress. Where would you go to get your facts?

If you decided to interview people who had been through a stressful situation—such as a tornado or fire—you could get useful information, although such people sometimes forget how they really felt at the time. Perhaps, then, you might try to *create* stress in people in order to see how they react. But this raises ethical problems, and most scientists agree that it is not good to scare or hurt people just to get information. Another approach, therefore, might be to find people who are undergoing stress anyway and to watch how they react.

This is exactly what was done by psychologists Walter Fenz and Seymour Epstein[10] when they studied people who were preparing to become parachutists. Many people today are nervous about *going up* in a plane, but to *get off* when the aircraft is 4000 feet above the ground can arouse sheer terror even among people who have volunteered for such activities! One report told how 2800 men had applied for training in sport parachuting (doing it for fun). After the first drop from a plane, *85 percent* of the trainees dropped out of the training program! Of those who came back, only a handful remained after the second or third jump.[11] Some of the trainees were so afraid that they refused to jump when the time came, others began to shake or vomit, and one man dealt with the pressure by falling into a deep sleep as the noisy airplane gained altitude.

All of these people were under stress because of fear. Fear is a tension which comes when we are in the presence or expect to be in the presence of danger or pain. Usually when we are afraid we also feel some uncertainty—we are not sure what, if anything, will happen to us. Sometimes it is not the dangers or pain which bother us, but it is the thoughts about what might happen which really put us under stress.

Few people experience the fear of jumping from an airplane, but there are many familiar fears which arise every day to put people under stress. Consider, for example, the fear which some of us have of heights, open spaces, boats, or being alone. And then there is the fear that a secret sin will be discovered, that our children will go astray, that our mate will be unfaithful, or that we won't be liked by others. The list is almost endless. Each of us probably fears something, and at times such fears can be intense and immobilizing.

Afraid of Failure

One of the most common and stressful fears in our success-oriented society is the fear that we might not make it—the fear that we will fail. Think about the person who isn't accepted into college, whose children don't turn out as expected, who fails to advance in the job, or whose marriage ends up on the rocks. All of us can feel with such situations because we've all failed at some time and we know how painful and stressful this can be. Many people will do almost anything to avoid such failure and the pain which it brings.

Why is failure so stressful? For one thing, we are taught almost from birth that getting ahead is important. Being successful is one of our major values, so we strive to achieve at all costs. But there is something more. Somehow we have come up with the idea that success is the same as personal worth. "If I'm successful," we think, "I must be worth something. If I don't succeed, perhaps I'm incapable or even worthless."

This thinking, which isn't very often stated so blatantly, drives some people to get ahead at all costs. They have to succeed to feel worthwhile. Others find excuses so they won't have to test themselves and risk failure. The student, for example, who doesn't bother to study has a built-in excuse for failure. "If I flunk out," he may conclude unconsciously, "I can always recognize that I didn't really try." It is possible, then, to maintain a belief in one's personal worth without having to be overwhelmed by failure.

The fear of not succeeding is a powerful motivator. It is also a very potent stress and one which bothers a lot of people.

Afraid of Closeness

Equally stressful, however, is the fear of getting too close to other people. This is what one writer has called our fear of love.[12]

To get close to another person is risky. What if the other person doesn't return our love, doesn't keep confidences, doesn't stay with us? What if we allow ourselves to get close to a neighbor, and then the neighbor moves away? Such experiences can be extremely painful, so in order to avoid the possibility of pain we are careful not to get too close to others.

Not too long ago my wife and I were browsing in a gift shop just off the boardwalk in Atlantic City. I spotted a little wooden plaque which impressed me so much that my wife later bought it for me as a gift. It read, "People are lonely because they build walls instead of bridges."

How do we build walls? By not showing our feelings, not touching, finding little things wrong with each other, starting petty arguments, or avoiding close contact. Why do we build these walls? Because we're afraid to get close—afraid that in such closeness our weaknesses will be revealed and we will have to risk being rejected or criticized. Closeness is one of the greatest and most stressful fears that modern man encounters.

PRESSURE AND CONFLICT

We also encounter pressure.

I feel it whenever I write a book. Some people can dash off a paragraph or two before they go to work every morning, but not me. I need a quiet place, room to spread out, a telephone that can be disconnected, and large blocks of uninterrupted time. All of this is difficult to get, so I usually plan my writing times several months in advance. During those precious days I take no speaking engagements, get out of town, and go to work with enthusiasm.

Very often, however, I still feel a time pressure. What if I don't get the book or article done when the publisher is expecting it? What if I'm interrupted in spite of all my precautions? I've come to realize that there are many things in life more important than writing books, but the pressure can still be there.

A few days ago I took some time off for lunch and went with my wife to a nearby restaurant. One the way home we made the mistake of stopping at a sidewalk sale. Soon I found myself rummaging through the bargains but feeling increasing pressure to get back to work. I also felt myself in a conflict. I wanted to linger over the merchandise but I also wanted to get into the car and hurry back to my desk.

Life is filled with pressures and conflicts like that. Sometimes we are pressured by deadlines, by our work, by the clock, or by the telephone. At other times we are pressured by people—a persistent salesman, our mate, our employers (or employees), professors (or students), the children (or our parents), or perhaps by a minister. Many times, however, the pressure is self-created. We set up goals for ourselves which may not be realistic, and then we feel pressure as we struggle to reach these goals.

An equally difficult struggle is that of trying to decide between two or more alternatives. This is called conflict, and it can be very stressful, especially if the alternatives are equally attractive. Will I buy a new car or fix up the old one? Will I go to Harvard or Yale? Will I eat the eclair with all its calories or will I sit and feel sorry for myself while everyone else indulges and I watch?

I once heard Elton Trueblood give a talk entitled "The

Agony of Choice." Making decisions isn't easy, he stated, especially when we are dealing with life-changing matters such as marriage, the purchase of a home, or a change of vocation. Together, pressures and conflict can put us under a great deal of stress.

STRESS AND THE SUPERNATURAL

The psychological textbooks don't say much about this, but if we believe in the supernatural, we must realize that forces outside our own control are able to put us under stress.

Let's go back to the example of Job, whom we discussed in Chapter 1. According to the Bible, Job's stresses were brought on by the Devil himself. Only a few years ago, most people rejected the idea of Satan's existence, but this view has begun to change. Widespread interest in demonology and the occult has convinced many previous skeptics that satanic forces may indeed exist and can create stress by interfering with the affairs of men.

For Christians, of course, this is hardly a new discovery. We are warned in the Bible about the Devil, who "prowls about like a roaring lion, seeking someone to devour."[13] Sometimes he appears as an angel in order to deceive people,[14] and we know that he is a shrewd schemer who controls a whole host of powerful spiritual forces who are in battle with mankind.[15]

This realization would be pretty stressful in itself were it not for the equal certainty of the power of God. When Satan brought stress into Job's life, it was only because God had given His divine permission.[16]

PAINFUL STRESS AND A LOVING GOD

But why would a loving God let human beings experience stress? That's a question that theologians have struggled with for centuries, and it is too big to be answered here. We do know, again from the Book of Job, that God sometimes has reasons for His actions which we are not able to understand right now. We also know, this time from the New Testament, that stresses sometimes bring glory to God, that they may come because of human disobedience, that they can straighten us out, and that they help us to develop patience. Strange as it may seem, these stresses are really an expression of divine love. They're something like surgery which hurts so we can get better, or like parental discipline which isn't pleasant at the time but which prepares us to face the future with less stress than we might have had otherwise.[17]

Stress, therefore, comes from a variety of sources, and not all stress is bad. Looking again to Dr. Selye,[18] we see a man who believes that stress can either be unpleasant (he calls that "distress") or it can be pleasant—the spice of life. One thing is certain: we cannot avoid stress completely, since any person who has no stress at all is dead! But we *can* do something to cope with unpleasant stress, and we can even benefit from those stresses which harm us and make life miserable. That is the topic of the next chapter.

Chapter 4
COPING WITH STRESS

Going to the hospital can be a very stressful situation, especially if you have never been there before and don't know what to expect. As a patient you are separated from family, daily routine, and familiar surroundings. Strangers in white uniforms take care of your body and even help with your most personal physical functions. Very often there is pain, body damage, loneliness, and perhaps the threat that you might die. It isn't easy to be hospitalized!

Over 25 years ago a Yale University psychologist named Irving Janis began a series of studies to find out how people react to the stress of major surgery.[1] In a large community hospital, patients were carefully interviewed before and after their operations. In addition, Dr. Janis talked with the nurses and doctors and had access to the hospital records. All of this led to the conclusion that the patients could be divided into three broad groups before surgery. The first group had high fear about the coming operation. These people were anxious, too nervous to sleep before the surgery, constantly worried, and afraid of all the things that could go wrong. Group two had moderate fear. They were tense and very inclined to ask questions about the operation, but they accepted reassurance from the medical staff, remained outwardly calm, and were able to read or engage in other diversions before surgery. Group three was the low fear group. They were constantly cheerful and optimistic about their operation, able to sleep soundly, and free of any observable signs of tension.

As you might expect, these three groups did not all come through the surgery with equal ease. The high-fear patients were as filled with anxiety after the operation as they were before. They complained about their treatment, refused to cooperate with nurses, and worried about their health. Surprising as it may seem, the low-fear patients (group three) had almost as much difficulty handling stress. Apparently they hadn't previously faced the fact that there would be considerable pain and discomfort. As a result, they too became angry, discouraged, uncooperative, and worried following surgery.

The people who handled the stress best were those who had had moderate fears before the operation. They had good morale after surgery, rarely complained, cooperated even when asked to submit to uncomfortable drainage tubes or injections, and recovered faster.

On the basis of this and other studies, Dr. Janis concluded that a person can cope with stress better when he or she has worried a little about it beforehand. Too much worry, or none at all, is harmful. But a little worry can be a healthy thing! Doctors and pastoral counselors have now come to see that talking to people before a stress arises— pointing out the dangers and giving realistic information— can make a big difference in helping people to cope when the stress finally comes.

Getting Inoculated Emotionally

Having an operation, however, is only one kind of stress, and this certainly isn't something which happens every day. Experts believe that any kind of stress can be handled better if we've had some time to think about it first. Dr. Janis calls this *emotional inoculation*.[2] Unlike an inoculation against measles or smallpox, it is not something solely physical. In emotional inoculation we provide realistic information about what might be coming, reassure the person that he can survive the stress, and then help him or her to think of means of self-protection. Without scaring their children, parents need to be giving this kind of emotional inoculation all the time. It's part of helping children to grow up.

COMMON STRESS REACTIONS

Whether we are emotionally immunized or not, all of us develop our own little bag of tricks for dealing with stress. Some of these work better than others, and what helps one person may be of no benefit to someone else.

Perhaps the three most common ways for handling stress are with humor (joking about it), tears (crying about it), and words (talking about it). All three of these can be overdone (for example, we can cry for hours), but in moderation all can be helpful. Each lets us release some of our tension, and if we talk to someone else we can often see our own problem in a new light and even get some assistance in finding a solution.

Nervous Mannerisms

Some people develop a variety of nervous gestures to help them cope with stress. Biting nails, chewing gum, snacking, or even masturbating can all help us to reduce tension. Regretfully, none of these deals with the source of our stress, and sometimes these bring new stresses of their own. Masturbation, for example, can create guilt, and even fingernail-biting can have unpleasant results.

After a talk on stress recently, a member of the audience approached me and suggested that we might go out for a cup of coffee. As he sat across the table I noticed that his fingernails had been bitten back almost as far as possible. "That's part of my problem," the man replied. "When I get under stress I start biting my fingernails until they bleed and really hurt." The nail-biting had helped to lessen the pain of stress, but another problem had risen as a result.

The Fat Is in Your Head

The same is true with overeating. Too much weight can create a great deal of stress, and as a result dozens of reducing diets are being marketed today. Very often it appears that the main reason Americans are overweight in the first place is that we have a great tendency to eat whenever we are nervous, afraid, or anxious. We may not eat much—perhaps a chocolate bar or some potato chips—but these high-carbohydrate foods add pounds quickly and, as we all know, it's a lot easier to add weight than to take it off!

Several years ago our family spent a year overseas, and I can still remember our reaction when we returned to New York. After our absence, what impressed us the most were the big cars (which we hadn't seen for awhile) and the large number of overweight people (which we hadn't noticed before).

In many cases stress and obesity go together, so that one solution is to find better ways of meeting the stress and dealing with the overweight. In all of this, mental attitude is very important—which is probably why Charlie Shedd wrote a book to convince people that "the fat is in your head."[3]

Religion

Within recent years there has been a widespread decline of interest in organized religion, both in North America and abroad. When stress arises, however, people who otherwise might never darken a church door turn to God in search of help. One is reminded of the frequently quoted statement that there are no atheists in foxholes.

For some people, belief in a deity—any deity—is encouraging and stress-reducing. Christians, however, believe that a personal, living God not only cares about the affairs of men but encourages us to bring our cares to Him, expecting that He will give help in time of trouble.[4] This leads many people to pray and read the Bible during times of stress—activities which can undoubtedly be stress-relieving.

Anger

Seemingly far removed from religion is anger. This is

one of the most common reactions to stress. Remember the frustration-aggression hypothesis that we discussed in the previous chapter? When we "blow our top" we might feel better for awhile, but our outbursts can hurt other people and make us feel guilty or ashamed.

A Change of Scene and Body

More helpful, perhaps, is the experience of taking a break, getting away from the stress, and doing something else for awhile. Here is the whole issue of hobbies, sports, and other diversions. Such activities can give physical exercise, provide relaxation, and enable us to come back to our stressful situation with a more balanced perspective. After a time away, problems can be seen in a new light, and as a result they may be a lot less stressful. There is also evidence that when we are in good physical condition we can withstand a virus, a spell of overwork, or even an argument better than the person who is out of shape.[5] And of course we feel better in general when our body is in good shape.

Within recent years many doctors have noted an interesting side effect in people who are not physically fit: chronic fatigue. Such people always feel tired and sluggish. Additional sleep makes them feel worse than before, and their whole lives drag. Studies have shown that the best cure for such stress is regular physical exercise. This releases pent-up emotions, helps us feel better, and enables us to approach our daily tasks with greater alertness and enthusiasm.[6]

We all know, however, that so-called physical and recreational activities aren't always recreational. When a highly competitive businessman takes up tennis to relieve his stress, the intense desire to win may actually create more stress than he faces at work! When hobbies or even vacations create more stress than they reduce, then these diversionary activities should be dropped while we look for something that can be *really* relaxing without getting us more tense.

Extra Work and Wandering Minds

Many people find that in times of stress it helps to keep busy. This is often true of widows. As part of their reaction to grief, they may get busy with activities that keep them useful, help them stay in contact with other people, and keep them from wallowing in self-pity or loneliness.

Of course this too can be overdone. I know a man who is one of the busiest people around, but the reason for this is apparent—his marriage is falling apart and his children are all rebellious. He has buried himself in work in order to avoid the stresses at home—stresses which can only get worse because a father is ignoring his family.

Though it is busy activity which takes this man away from a tense situation, it is also possible to withdraw from others without even leaving the room. My students do it all the time, and so do many bored people in church on Sunday mornings. By letting our minds wander, we avoid the boredom of the present situation and we amuse ourselves with something more interesting.

Recently I read a report which suggested that half-an-hour of boredom can burn up more nervous energy and create more tension than a whole day of work. If this is true, it shows the importance of cultivating new interests and broadening our horizons.

Withdrawing into Ourselves

But for many people a turning to new and creative activities seems impossible. For them it is too painful and threatening to face stress head-on, so they withdraw emotionally and physically into a bizarre world of mental illness. At times such people become discouraged or deeply depressed, and with this may come the threat of suicide as the ultimate escape.

Withdrawing into a Bottle

Of course few of us reach the stage of mental illness, and

rarely do we seriously consider suicide (although probably everyone has toyed with the idea at some time). A more common form of withdrawal is by using drugs.

We have become a pill-popping nation, convinced that there must be some drug available for solving every human problem, whether physical or psychological. Recently a cartoon appeared showing a distraught mother listening to the words of her young son. "Gee, Mom," the boy says, "when the lady on TV gets irritable *she* takes a pill. Then she gets real nice again."

Such pills, as we all know, can be very helpful in producing relaxation. This is especially true if they are taken infrequently or under the recommendation of a physician. Taking pills such as tranquilizers can help us to tackle life more enthusiastically, but they don't really teach us anything about how to cope with stress. They dull but do not eliminate the stress problem. If people begin to rely on drugs to maintain stability or get an emotional "high" (especially if the drugs are illegal), then the getting and taking of drugs becomes a *source* of stress rather than a *solution* to the stress.

This can also be true of a legal drug like alcohol. Alcoholism has become our number one drug problem, and it's a problem on the increase. For many people, a drink before dinner can help to relieve stress, at least temporarily, but this opens the door for another drink, and another. In the beginning alcohol may relieve tension, but for some people the body develops a physiological dependence on the drug. More and more alcohol is needed to satisfy the body and to eliminate the unpleasant side effects of drinking. What began as a *stress-reliever* soon becomes a major *stress-producer* in the drinker and in his or her family.

WHICH IS BEST FOR YOU?

Most of us have developed our own techniques for coping with stress: humor, crying, talking, nervous mannerisms, eating, drinking, anger, hobbies, vacations, sports, withdrawal, drugs. To this we might add the mental games that most of us use at least occasionally—finding excuses for our failures, blaming somebody else, trying to hide our inadequacies, or withdrawing into a fantasy world of television. Clearly some of these (like talking about a problem) are healthy reactions to stress, while others (like drinking) can create more stress than they relieve. How can we decide which of these techniques is best?

To a large extent the answer is found in our past experience. What has helped us before is likely to be an effective stress-reducer in the future. We learn from experience (and from our parents) what works and what doesn't work. We discover very early in life that some behavior (like crying or sharing a problem with another person) is quite acceptable in some families and communities, but unacceptable in others. Even personality may make a difference. Dr. Aaron T. Beck, a University of Pennsylvania Medical School psychiatrist, suggests that some of us tend to be "sensitizers," while others are what he calls "repressors."[7]

Sensitizers are overly sensitive to tension. They are aware of every little change in their physiology—back pain, stomach tension, headaches, etc. This awareness can aggravate their troubles, creating worry on top of their original stress. *Repressors*, in contrast, are never aware of being up-tight. Friends may know they're tense, and business associates may observe the tension, but the individual is oblivious to his tension until he or she has a heart attack or develops a bleeding ulcer.

Much of this suggests that reactions to stress are largely individualistic and automatic. Most of us don't think about our stress reactions very often. We cope as best we can with the techniques we've developed and hope that these will work. In many cases they do work, but as the stresses of our society increase, the haphazard approach to handling stress will succeed less and less. Already thousands—probably hundreds of thousands—of people are suffering unnecessary physical pain and mental turmoil because their coping techniques are not adequate to handle the increasing stresses of life.

It might come as a disappointment for you to realize that there is no "best technique" for everyone, and that there is no magic formula which can eliminate all unpleasant stress forever. But there *are* things we can do beyond a random reliance on the common coping reactions which each of us has developed in the past.

TAKING INVENTORY

Simple as it may seem, there can be great value in sitting down, perhaps with a piece of paper for taking notes, and asking yourself some questions: Why am I uptight? What, specifically, is causing my stress? Is there anything I can do to tackle the problem? What would be my first step? Have I dealt with a similar situation in the past? If so, would the former solution work now? Suppose I can't resolve this stress-producing problem—could I still go on living? Might I be creating the problem myself or at least be keeping it going because I'm getting some benefits from it (like sympathy, attention, and days home from work)?

Taking stock of your situation like this can help get your problem in perspective, and such review often brings new ideas for coping. If such a self-examination doesn't work very well, try it with a friend, whose noninvolvement may help you get a clearer picture of what is happening.

Often a self-examination like this will lead you to a reexamination of your priorities. What is *really* important in life? Do we have to yield to every demand on our time? The theology students in my classes have learned a lot about Biblical languages, but I try to convince them that there is one English word that is more important to them than all their Hebrew and Greek vocabulary put together. It's the word "no." Sometimes we have to turn down an invitation or opportunity even though we would like to accept it. We must recognize that we will never accomplish everything that we hope to accomplish, so we should set some realistic goals, arrange them in priority, and go from there.

In an in-depth study of children, one researcher discovered that the youngsters would narrow the field and start working on their stresses one at a time.[8] This is a good policy. Research shows that a single stress almost always takes priority over all others. It is best to work first on that which is most disturbing and move to the others later.[9] Incidentally, this is a good guideline for tackling work—start first with the most unpleasant task, so that you get it over as quickly as possible.

It is important to realize that there may be some pressure-building responsibilities that you can get rid of. A friend of mine recently found himself in the hospital as the result of a general physical collapse. The doctor's advice was concise—"Cut back on your activities. You're trying to do everything and are wearing yourself out." If you can't keep your house clean and your garden productive, decide which has to go. If Kiwanis and Rotary take too much time, drop one. If you feel pressure to read all the magazines which come into your house, cancel a subscription or two. If business is too hectic, hire some help or cut back before a heart attack does the job for you.

In all of this, be specific. "I'm going to spend Friday nights with my wife and kids" is much more realistic and attainable than "I'm losing my family so I'd better become a better family man." The former is specific and manageable; the latter is too vague.

BUILDING SKILLS

Have you ever had to take a driver's test in order to get your license? This can be a very stressful experience. I was thinking about this when I drove into the examiner's station recently to take my road test—that part of the examination where you are observed as you drive around the city or a specially constructed course. As we drove I had an interesting discussion with the examiner, who was quick to inform me that he had a stressful time himself. "We have an average of three accidents a day," he told me, "mostly because of foolish mistakes made by nervous drivers."

There is, I suspect, one way that people can reduce some of the tension connected with the driver's test—they can learn to drive. By developing skills they are less likely to make mistakes. Much of education is teaching people how to be skillful, and this reduces the stress when we have to perform.

All of this, however, involves risk. Trying something new, daring to be different, making a difficult decision—all of this exposes us to the prospect of failure and of being wrong. This, as we have seen earlier, is very threatening, so much so that some people refuse to take the chance. They would rather be unskilled and under stress than risk the added stress that comes with failure.

What can be done to reduce the risk? First we can get a realistic expectation of what's coming. Find out what is involved in learning your new skill and try to determine whether you can do it. Recognize, for example, that it isn't easy to learn how to drive when you're over fifty, but it *can* be done. People do it every day. Recognize too that our mental attitude very often determines what will happen in a learning situation. Students who are told that they are incapable and likely to fail usually do fail. But it works the other way, too. Positive thinking ("I *can* do it") often leads to success.

Second, in learning skills try to get the best and most realistic experience possible. As a very young child I began piano lessons in a class where everyone had cardboard duplicates of the keyboard. It wasn't very realistic and I lasted exactly one lesson. In learning to counsel, my students are given opportunity to practice on each other, and then they work with real counselees, closely supervised by an instructor. This is more realistic than reading a book about counseling techniques.

Third, try to avoid giving in to your own desires for

comfort. It is much easier to take a tranquilizer than it is to really come to grips with a stress, but the pill brings only temporary relief. We all know of people who take pain-dulling medications while they put off seeing the doctor about some problem. Usually these people make excuses for their behavior ("It's probably nothing serious," "It will go away if I wait long enough"), and sometimes while they're waiting the problem gets worse. What is true of physical illness can also apply to psychological stress.

There are times, however, when waiting may be the best policy. If the risk is too great and there seems almost no chance of success, or if the pressures are so great that you can't do anything new for the present, or if there is a real likelihood that the problem may pass on its own, then to do nothing may be a good way to cope. Very often, however, as an excuse to do nothing we convince ourselves that each of these conditions is true. To make sure of the facts, it is best to talk things over with a friend or counselor.

Indeed, the encouragement and perspective of others can be central in coping with stress. Based on studies of people under intense pressure, one psychologist concluded that "those who survive longest seem to be those who expend most energy in helping and supporting others."[10]

MAKING CHANGES

When we have taken an inventory of what is going on and have developed some needed skills, we are well on our way to coping with stress at its source. Briefly stated, this coping involves three reactions. First we change our environment. Shifting workloads, taking up a hobby, dropping out of some club, changing our schedules—all of these are ways in which we can change the world around to reduce stress.

Second, we can change our perspective. Often there is nothing we can do to change the world around us. Economic depressions, rising prices, terminal illness, death, dangerous weather conditions—these are beyond our control as individuals, but we can learn to look at them from a different point of view. Too often in the midst of stress we lose our perspective, so that things look blacker than they really are. Here is where a long, hard look at a situation (best done with the help of a more objective friend or counselor) can help us get a more balanced point of view. This can make us less up-tight and even help us to see solutions.

Third, we can change our environment by altering the body that is taking the stress. Simple things like getting sufficient rest, exercise, a balanced diet, or the shedding of extra pounds can enable us to rise more effectively to the pressures of modern living.

In all of this we must remember that some stresses are here to stay. To watch your mate die, for example, and to experience the indescribable loneliness of grief is a stress situation which cannot be dealt with by applying the advice given in a few paragraphs of some book. Such stress requires a complete life readjustment. It involves changing your world, your view of life, and yourself. It necessitates the loving support and encouragement of friends. It takes vast amounts of time and effort. And it is best done with divine help.

USING YOUR SPIRITUAL RESOURCES

Religion is not very popular in our era, but even secular psychiatry is coming to recognize that spiritual influences can be very important in helping us handle stress. One of the major needs facing people under stress today, writes Dr. Jules H. Masserman of Northwestern University's Department of Psychiatry, is "some kind of belief, religious or philosophical, to bolster our conviction that man is not just another animal."[11]

The Bible is very explicit in teaching that men and women are more than animals. We are valuable creatures, made in the image of God, given control over the earth, and endowed with so much freedom that we can even disobey God. And that is precisely what each of us has done.

If God is really holy, as the Bible teaches, then He can't wink at our sin. In fact, because of our sin we are each condemned to permanent alienation from God. But the news isn't all bad. In fact, the good news of Christianity is that God cares. He sent His perfect Son, Jesus, to die in punishment for our sins—past, present, and future—and God has made it possible for us to live with Him forever following our physical death.

We are still free to reject God's offer and go our own way, for God doesn't force anything on us. We can even try to work our way into God's favor, but the Bible warns that this won't succeed. It is by confessing our sins, acknowledging that we have fallen far short of God's standards, and giving our lives to Jesus Christ in personal commitment that we become God's children by adoption into His family.[12]

It would be misleading and wrong to imply that this is the solution to all our problems. Christians are not immune from stress, but they can have intimate contact with a loving, powerful God who gives strength and help in times of difficulty. This was the experience of the Apostle Paul in prison and of John banished to the Isle of Patmos. This has been the experience of believers for centuries, and it can be true for us.

Job's Response to Stress

Consider once again the case of Job. Most of us probably couldn't take as much stress as he faced, and it almost overwhelmed Job himself. But this godly man dealt with his stresses by reacting in three somewhat unusual ways.

First, Job worshipped. At first this seems most unusual, but it isn't really strange at all if we believe that God is all-powerful and is aware of what is going on in the world. If He *isn't* powerful and all-knowing, He isn't God at all. Job realized this, saw that God had to be still in control, and gave praise in the midst of despair. We are instructed to do likewise.[13]

Second, Job obeyed. It isn't easy to seek God's direction when you're under pressure. More often people turn away in bitterness and vacillate between anger, guilt, and dependence on the Lord. Job had a struggle about yielding, but he did not sin despite all his stress, nor did he blame God, even when encouraged to do so by a nagging wife.[14]

Third, Job accepted. He faced the reality of his stress, accepted the fact that he had a problem, and determined to do something about it. Such acceptance is always the first step in meeting stress effectively.

To accept does not mean that we have to enjoy something. I have a friend who recently lost his wife of fifty years. He is not enjoying his loneliness and grief, but he accepts the fact that his wife has been taken and that he must make the difficult readjustment of living on his own.

To accept, furthermore, does not mean that we never question. Job accepted his stresses as coming from God, but that didn't stop his struggle to understand why. God has given us inquiring minds, which He expects us to use. Sometimes we don't get an immediate answer—Job didn't—but there is nothing wrong with trying to comprehend the reasons for our problems.

Finally, to accept does not mean that we do nothing. Sometimes people give up in the face of stress. They shrug their shoulders in a "what's-the-use" attitude and withdraw into inactivity. Let me mention my widower friend again. "Part of me is gone," he stated after the funeral. "I won't be as efficient as before. But I plan to press on as best I can with the skills, opportunities, and life that I still have." This is true, realistic acceptance.

Our Response to Stress

How do we cope with stress? Clearly there can be a variety of answers to that question, because there are a variety of coping techniques. In some way, at least partially, most of these techniques work to relieve the pressures of life. But the place to start is by returning to our Creator, casting our burdens on Him and fully expecting that we will be sustained and helped, just as the Bible promises. When we do this the stresses of life help us grow. They become not merely obstacles to be overcome, but steps which enable us to profit and grow in maturity.

Part Two

ENCOUNTERING STRESS:

Day-to-Day Coping

Chapter 5
EVERYDAY STRESS

"There was no way to write about it that night. It would have been an indignity to have done that to people trying to find out where they had been in crisis."

The words were that of a newspaper reporter trying to describe the reactions of people who had survived a train wreck. The tragedy had happened suddenly, just a few days before. Due to the failure of a warning system, a morning commuter train on its way to Chicago had plowed into another train, killing many people and injuring others. So unusual was the impact that some survivors escaped unhurt while people in the next seat were killed.

You don't walk away from that kind of experience unscathed, even if you think you have steel control of your nerves. People feel helpless, overwhelmed, and happy to be alive, yet guilty because they were spared. For this reason a local hospital offered to give "survivor counseling" to people who escaped the train wreck unhurt. The newspaper reporter came along to watch:

> I was an interloper, looking for a story. There was one, of course. People in that tight little room were just coming to grips with the thing that had happened to them. Others had died, they had made it out.
> "I went back to school the next day," this girl with soft brown hair was saying. "They asked me to talk about it. They said, 'Oh, it must have been terrible.' I couldn't talk about it. I couldn't tell them how terrible it was. They couldn't know. . . ."
> And she turned to the girl next to her and wept. They were tiny girls, both of them, weeping together. Their feet did not even touch the floor from the couch they sat on.

A soldier leaned over. His sister had died on that train. He had come home to help his family. "I think I know what it was like, maybe," he said. "In Viet Nam. . . ."

They looked at him doubtfully, accepted him a little. But he hadn't been there, in their tragedy.

A middle-aged woman across the room started crying softly.

"When they started taking them out, the people who had been sitting next to me, there were pieces of them. They were unreal. But they had been sitting next to me."

"Nobody told us what to do," a man in a workman's shirt said. It was like an obligato. It melded with the others. It did not interrupt.

"I waited and I stood there and I saw the hands and faces pressed against the window and I couldn't do anything. Nobody told us what to do."

No anger. Just helplessness. And the help in talking to one another. They had all been there.[1]

SURVIVING THE STRESSES OF LIFE

Few of us ever take survivor counseling, but then most of us have never been in a train wreck or plane crash. We all experience the stress of life, however, and sometimes, in their desire to observe the more spectacular stresses, researchers forget the little things that put so many of us under pressure. The sickness of a child in the night, the unexpected death of a neighbor, the failure of your check to arrive on time, the financial struggles of buying a house, the theft of your kid's bike, the pressure of a tough exam, the illegitimate pregnancy of your teenage daughter, the disappointment of not getting a raise—these and thousands of others are the everyday stresses of life. They almost never make the headlines, and sometimes they are kept locked within the four walls of your house. They may even stay locked within your brain, but they are stresses nevertheless.

In this and the next several chapters we will look at some of the more common stresses that people face in their journey through life. We will begin with the problem of pressure.

PRESSURE

In order to function efficiently, the human nervous system requires that there be continual stimulation coming from the environment. When people are put in darkened rooms where they cannot see, hear, or talk to anyone, they soon develop pathological symptoms. Their minds begin to crack under the monotony.

Such is not the problem for most of us today. Living at the end of the twentieth century is a fast-paced experience, for we have somehow developed the idea that we ought to be going all the time. As a result we dash from project to project, from meeting to meeting, and from idea to idea—all the time wondering, as we flop into a chair at the end of the day, why with all our activity we still didn't get much done.

Writing several years ago, Sebastian de Grazia suggested that "perhaps you can judge the inner health of a land by the capacity of its people to do nothing—to lie abed, musing, to amble about aimlessly, to sit having coffee, because whoever can do nothing, letting his thoughts go where they may, must be at peace with himself."[2] If there is any truth to this, many people in our land are not in a very good state of inner health. We are constantly under pressure from two sources.

Two Kinds of Pressure

First there is outer pressure, that which comes from the world around. The demands of employers, children, professors, salesmen, or neighbors can all be stressful. And this starts early. Consider, for example, the pressures of Little League (which affect the parents as well as the kids), piano lessons, and (what is becoming more and more of a problem) the pressures that come from school. There are demands for children to read earlier, perform at a higher level, get more work done, spend more days in school, or be more physically fit. Even in the early grades the pressures can be tremendous, and some students can't cope. During a visit to Hong Kong I was told that the major physical problem among high school students was ulcers, created in part by the pressure to get into the few openings at the universities. Stress in North America may have different causes, but it is no less intense, and this may indicate why the leading cause of death among college students is suicide.

Equally demanding are inner pressures. Here are the in-grained beliefs that we must perform well, meet other people's expectations, accomplish some lofty goals in life that we believe are important, turn out model children, keep a clean house, finish any book we start, answer the telephone whenever it rings, be well-liked and well-rounded, get A's on our tests, etc. The list, of course, could go on for pages. From our parents, our teachers, our religious leaders, and our own deliberations we have set up a list of demands which we put on ourselves, and then we spend our lives under the constant pressure of trying to meet our own expectations.

Managing Time

What can be done about pressure? It's difficult for an individual to do much about the rapid pace of society, but we *can* do something about our own mental attitude within that society. Recently Alan Lakein, an authority on time management, was interviewed in a news magazine and gave a number of practical suggestions for the management of pressures.[3]

We waste 80 percent of our time, Mr. Lakein reported, even though we are perpetually busy. The problem comes because we don't know what we want to do with our lives (the problem of priorities), we don't know how to reach our goals once they are determined, and we have a great tendency to procrastinate once we do know how to attain our goals. To meet these problems the stress expert has several recommendations.

First, ask yourself these questions: What are my lifetime goals? How would I like to spend the next five years? How would I live if I knew that in six months I would be killed in an accident? The answers to these questions can be helpful in goal-setting. The Christian would want to preface all of this with the question, "What do I believe God wants me to be doing with my life?" In answering these questions we should get a better perspective on our goals and priorities.

Next Mr. Lakein suggests that we divide our activities into priorities. A is most important, B is next, and C takes the lowest priority. At the start of each day make a list of the things you need to do, and concentrate on getting the A things done. It appears that most of us have a period during the day when we are most efficient. This is "prime time," and it is during this time that we should be doing activities of prime importance.

Does all of this work? The time expert claims it does. It lets us get more done and it reduces the pressures in our lives.

Pressure and Your State of Mind

Notice that a lot of our coping with pressure depends on our state of mind. It is easy to convince ourselves that we can't control our busyness. Without much thought we've accepted the debatable ideas that leisure is bad, that time is money, or that pressure is insurmountable.

Perhaps we need to think again about Jesus. He taught for only three years on a schedule which appeared to be exceptionally demanding. But He never got flustered and never seemed rushed—and still He changed the course of history. What was His secret of handling pressure? First, He knew His priorities—why He was here and what He wanted to accomplish. Second, He had His values straight. He sought to do the work God had given Him, and He wasn't caught up in the drive for status, money, or power. Third, He spent time every day meditating alone with His

Father. In this way Jesus kept things in perspective. Is there any reason why we can't do the same?

MONOTONY

At the risk of oversimplification, we could probably categorize people from our society in two broad camps—those who are always busy and those who don't have anything to do. The first group is pressured, the second is bored, and neither is able to understand the other very well! I have no difficulty placing myself in the busy group, but there was a time when it was otherwise. Tucked in the shelves of my library are several old schoolbooks with my handwritten inscription: "Bored of Education." Those days in grade school weren't very stimulating!

Like pressure, boredom can be very stressful. Our usual reaction is to look for something to do or to fantasize—trying to stimulate ourselves mentally. This, however, doesn't work for very long, because even fantasy and creativity require input from the environment around. Monotony can make us feel restless, anxious, useless, irritable, and tired. It can also reduce our efficiency. During the Second World War it was discovered that sailors whose job it was to watch the radar for enemy ships could only remain alert for a short time. Very quickly they got bored and somehow failed to spot new signs on the radar screen. A similar effect of boredom has been seen in assembly line operations, where employees are less efficient unless they frequently change from job to job during the day.

Soap Operas and the Boredom of Life

Many people seem to deal with their monotony by withdrawing into the fantasy world of television. Exciting quiz shows that enable people to earn fabulous prizes, soap operas that provide family-type drama, and programs steeped in sex and violence provide both escape and stimulation for homebound women, bored children, and men with uninspiring jobs.

Once again, the problem appears to be one of goals and priorities. If the job has no challenge, if there are few friends or hobbies, and if there is no possibility for change, then it is easy to give up and forget one's frustration by withdrawing into the world of television or alcohol.

Tackling Monotony

It is difficult to really tackle monotony, because the bored person often doesn't know what to do and is convinced that there is no way out of his situation. To reevaluate our goals in life and to plan some new activities for reaching these goals is one step in the right direction. If one part of our life is monotonous and unchangeable (our work, for instance) we need to find other activities—church clubs or social service, for example—which give us something interesting to do and offset the boring part of our lives which cannot be changed. Then we can learn to be creative. There are always things to do around the house, magazines to read, or people to see and help—all of which can provide variety and greater meaning to life.

All of this requires effort, however. When we're steeped in monotony it's easy for us to slip into a laziness which decreases our activity and makes our boredom worse. Here again, the helpful advice of a friend can often enable us to see pathways to greater variety in life than we can see by ourselves.

LOW SELF-ESTEEM

Do you remember the Old Testament account of Moses and the burning bush? Moses was born in Egypt of Jewish parents at a time when all male Hebrew babies had been ordered killed. In an attempt to save the baby's life, Moses' parents had hidden their infant son in a little floating basket near the edge of the Nile River. It was here that the baby was found by the king's daughter, who took Moses back to the palace and raised him as a prince.

When he reached adulthood, Moses intervened one day in a dispute between a Jew and an Egyptian. The Egyptian was killed in the fight, and Moses, fearing for his life, ran to the land of Midian, where he married and settled down as a shepherd.

Then one day God spoke to Moses out of a burning bush and told him to go back to Egypt, stand up to the king, and lead the oppressed Hebrews out from under Egyptian bondage. Immediately Moses began to make excuses. "I'm a nobody," he said. "People in Egypt will not believe God sent me, and furthermore I'm a very poor speaker who will get all tongue-tied in the king's presence."

Clearly God had a plan for delivering His people, but Moses had a problem. It was a problem of low self-esteem. Apparently the man by the burning bush felt inferior, inadequate, and overwhelmed by what God was asking. In essence, Moses was saying, "I'm no good. I can't do it!"

Two Worlds

In a very real sense, each of us lives in two worlds. One of these is public, seen by others. How we act, what we say, where we go—these can all be observed by anyone who wants to look. The other world, however, is private. It includes what we think and how we feel. Very often our inner and outer worlds work together. We say what we mean, express how we feel, do what we want, and act in accordance with our conscience.

But what about those times when there is conflict between our public and private worlds? This can create a tension with which we are all familiar. We receive a gift which we are expected to greet with great delight and thanks (the public world), but inwardly we may neither like the present nor want it (the private world). Someone invites us to dinner. Socially we are expected to indicate that we would really like to do this, but inwardly we may be thinking how much we don't want to accept or how we dislike spending time with the would-be host.

When these two worlds are in conflict we try to bring peace, either by changing our outer behavior (e.g., "I'm sorry but we cannot come for dinner") or by altering our inner thinking ("they're not all *that* bad, and we can probably leave early"). Since the two worlds try to reach a balance, it is often possible by looking at public behavior to get a clue about another person's private world. Consider shyness, for example.

Shyness

Inwardly, the shy person thinks that he or she isn't very good at meeting new people, making new friends, or saying and doing the right thing in social situations. The shy person feels self-conscious, afraid of what others will think, concerned about being disliked, and convinced of his or her inadequacy and incompetence. Surprising as it may seem, this is a very common problem which is based on the private evaluations that we make of ourselves.[4]

How, then, does the shy person act in the public world where others can see? Very often with silence, especially in the presence of strangers or members of the opposite sex. Sometimes the shy person looks away from people or even tries to take refuge in books or some other private project. When it is necessary to speak, the shy person does so in a quiet voice. The withdrawn actions on the outside point to the feelings of inadequacy within.

Why are people shy? Is shyness a personality trait that some people retain for life? Recently a group of researchers interviewed over eight hundred college students in an attempt to answer these questions.[5] It was found that shy people feel very inadequate and are excessively concerned about competition, individual success, and not being liked. They are hesitant to move boldly into the world lest they fail and experience an even greater sense of inferiority.

These people have a poor opinion of themselves, a low self-esteem.

Selfism

It is not just shy people who see themselves as being inadequate. Some people who ooze charm and exude self-confidence are really very insecure and inadequate but are hiding behind a mask of joviality and outer friendliness.

Dr. Maurice E. Wagner, a professional counselor in Los Angeles, has written a whole book about this common problem of low self-esteem.[6] Almost always, he suggests, there are three characteristics of low self-esteem: the feeling that we don't belong, the feeling that we are worthless, and the feeling that we are incompetent. All three of these are expressions of what Dr. Wagner calls selfism—an inner, self-centered concern about how other people will react to us. This is especially uncomfortable and stressful when other people expect us to do one thing, when we fear that we can't do what is expected, and when we think that our inability may cause us to lose respect in the eyes of others.

This was the problem of Moses. God expected him to lead the children of Israel out of Egypt, but Moses didn't think he could do it, and he was afraid that if he tried he might fail. Moses had a low self-esteem, a problem of selfism, which caused him to make excuses in an attempt to get out of doing what God wanted.

At times this kind of stress hits almost everyone. When I write a book, for example, I know that my publisher and many of my readers expect something worthwhile. "But what if I fail?" I might ask myself. "What if the book gets bad reviews? What if people think it's too superficial or too hard to understand? What might this do to my reputation or my career?" It is this kind of inner struggle which can almost petrify children in the presence of their parents' demands, students in the classroom, employees at work, or housewives in front of the Women's Missionary Society. This is not a matter of *being* inadequate or inferior. It's a problem of *believing* that we won't meet our own and someone else's expectations and that as a result we will suffer a loss of prestige.

Tension

This conscious or unconscious concern about our ability to perform lies at the basis of another very common stress—feelings of tension. We sometimes speak of *nervous* tension, tense situations, or of tensions between people, but as Jay Adams correctly points out, tension exists only in the muscles.[7] It is a physical reaction, a contracting of the muscles, which occurs in all of us when we are threatened. In one respect this tension is good. It prepares us for emergencies and keeps us alert. When the tension persists, however, we become restless, fidgety, and unable to concentrate. We might bite our nails or show other nervous mannerisms, and very often there are such physical reactions as backaches, chest pains, stiff necks, or headaches. One recent report has suggested that roughly half of all headaches come from a muscle tension which results from the pressures of daily living.[8]

Reducing Tension

The best way to reduce this tension is to relax the muscles, but how can we do that? Aspirin helps, and so may tranquilizers, but these only dull the pain and make us more inclined not to face the basis of the problem.

The real problem is that we have let ourselves become too much convinced that our personal worth depends upon the evaluations of other people. I am valuable, we conclude, only if I perform well, look good, am well-liked, and am accepted by others. Notice what we have done. We have staked our personal worth on the opinions of others. Lest we be rejected by other people, some of us retreat into shyness, some of us make excuses to protect ourselves like Moses, and some of us develop a muscle tension to keep us always alert. All of this indicates a low self-esteem, low because it depends upon our own evaluation and the evaluation that comes from other people.

Building Self-Esteem

We would be free from a lot of stress if we could somehow get out from under this fear of being rejected. One solution is to use a little positive thinking. Here we can focus on our strengths, convincing ourselves that the opinions of others aren't all that important, and setting our minds to the goal of succeeding. This sounds good, but regretfully it doesn't always work. In fact, sometimes we even have the ingrained idea that a low self-esteem is something desirable.

I once held a seminar for businessmen and got this interesting note from a member of the audience:

> I suffer from a poor self-concept. I had a devout, godly mother who always equated success and self-esteem with pride (which she considered to be the worst of sins). It has always been difficult for me, in any part of my life, to imagine myself being successful in any way. I have been on guard against self-esteem to an alarming degree. This has led at times to depression, morbid introspection and lack of good work habits. I am trying to succeed by not being successful![9]

This man needed to realize that a low view of himself is not a mark of spirituality; it is evidence of an unbalanced theology. According to the Bible it is God who made us in the divine image, loves us, sent His Son to die for us, made it possible for us to come to Him, gave us spiritual gifts, empowered us with His Holy Spirit, and has given us the opportunity to serve Him by serving others. All of this shows God's respect for individuals like you and I. He didn't make us robots who had neither freedom nor dignity. He created us free people who can reject or serve Him at will.

Moses quickly learned that it wasn't he who had to stand up to the Egyptian Pharaoh and lead an army of Hebrews out into the promised land. That could have been immobilizing! Instead, it was God who was going to act, using Moses as His instrument. Remember, God said to Moses, "Who has made a man's mouth? Or who makes him dumb or deaf, or seeing or blind? Is it not I, the Lord? . . .I am the Lord, and I will bring you out from under the burdens of the Egyptians."[10]

As human beings we have nothing to boast about in ourselves; our strengths, gifts, abilities, and successes all come from God. He is making each believer into something valuable and worthwhile to Him. Our job, therefore, is not to knock ourselves down, or to conclude that our worth depends on whether we succeed and are accepted in the eyes of other people. Neither is it for us to go through life moaning "poor little me—I'm no good." That's not spirituality. That's like saying, "God goofed when He made me."

Instead, we must freely acknowledge our strong and weak points, receive each with gratitude, develop the abilities and gifts that we *do* have, and go on to build a positive view of ourselves based on what God has done and is doing in our lives. Of course we are concerned about the opinions of other people, but this isn't the basis for our self-worth. We are valuable and can hold our heads high because of the work of God in us.

FROM MOSES TO MODERNS

Many things have changed in the centuries since Moses was alive. As a people, we are healthier—but more worried about things like cancer and heart attacks. We are more mobile and can get around easier—but we are more quickly scattered, lonely, and isolated from close interpersonal relationships. We are more aware of the world because of our mass media and telecommunications—but we are also more concerned about earthquakes, pollution, crime, violence, and the trauma of disasters, like train wrecks. With advances in psychology and medicine, we know more about man's capabilities and potential—but we probably worry more about financial loss, political turmoil, and not succeeding in life.

Perhaps it is not surprising, then, that stress has become a part of our everyday lives, and the pursuit of tranquility has become a national obsession. Recently a psychologist did an in-depth study of the things that make people happy. He studied the influence of money, knowledge, work, and status, but concluded when the results were in that by far the most important ingredient for happiness is love.[11]

Do you remember what Jesus said about that? God *is* love. It is from Him that all love comes. He loves us and wants us to love one another. Moses learned of God's love centuries ago, and this divine God has remained unchanged since the voice came from the burning bush.

We will continue to experience stress in our daily lives. It's part of being alive. But we can cope effectively, especially if we are honest enough to think about our stresses and their causes; brave enough to acknowledge our strengths and weaknesses; dedicated enough to examine our priorities, goals, and values frequently; humble enough to realize that our strengths and successes come from God;[12] alert enough to develop a positive self-esteem based on God's promises in the Bible; and flexible enough to keep reexamining ourselves so that we can grow in the light of our experiences and increased understanding. That is a tall order! But it is possible for everyone because we have a God of love who helps us to meet the stresses of daily living.

Chapter 6
FAMILY STRESS

It's an interesting collection—the books and articles on marriage and the family that I've collected during the past eight or ten years. The titles alone can give a pretty good picture of what's going on:

Families and Pressure
Family Stress Increasing
Is the American Family in Danger?
Can the Family Survive the 20th Century?
The Family in Transition: Re-thinking Marriage
How to Be Happy Though Married
The American Way of Marriage: Divorce and Remarriage
Anthropologist Urges Family Substitute
Is the Family Doomed?
The Crisis of Family Disintegration
Marriage—How to Leave It and Still Love It

Clearly, something is wrong with the great state of matrimony. That which has held firm as a rock for centuries appears to be coming unglued. The divorce rate is climbing, sex apart from marriage appears to be increasing, traditional views about male and female roles are changing, and a host of stresses from outside the home are forcing many families to crumble and fall apart. "My parents had their thirtieth wedding anniversary last week," a friend told me recently. "The whole family came together for a reunion—and we got into a big family fight!" Such reports are saddening, but they don't surprise us anymore.

Earlier in this century, sociologists noted that the family was the great shock absorber of society. If you had a problem, you could always take it home and expect to find support and encouragement in the midst of a stable and loving environment. In addition, the family provided a place for relaxation, education, and religious instruction. Edith Schaeffer, writing in a warm and moving book, described the family as "a shelter in the time of storm" and a place where there can be room for creativity, close human relationships, teaching, and the building of memories.[1]

But for thousands of people the memories aren't very pleasant and the family is neither very stable nor very important. "Home, sweet home" becomes little more than a center where independently willed people with a host of outside interests come together to sleep, grab a late bite to eat, catch a TV show, and get the laundry done. The father is often absent or too tired after work to get much involved in family activities. Many mothers are gone too, working to supplement the family income or involved in activities which they find more fulfilling than homemaking. Left on their own, the kids get caught up in a variety of school, community, and other peer group activities. Sometimes they get into trouble, and they often spend long hours watching fights and murders on television—that impersonal machine which has become the cheapest, most harmful, and number one babysitter in America.

Many young people give up on their home life and run away. It is estimated that one million persons take off every year, half of them under seventeen and mostly girls. Others stick it out in homes where frustration and bitterness explode at times in verbal abuse and physical violence. And what about the adults in the family? They are forsaking each other in increasing rates, flocking to divorce courts or else staying at home and surrounding themselves with emotional walls of protection and isolation.

THE FAMILY: PAST, PRESENT, AND FUTURE

Everybody knows how families were structured in the past. Father was the head of the home, often an austere presence whose word was authority. Mother was the obedient, subservient wife who ran the household and brought up children who would be seen and not heard. Sex was never mentioned, hard work and moral purity were sacred values, and when problems arose they were rarely if ever mentioned outside the home. Marriages weren't always happy, but they usually lasted.

Such a picture of the family is certainly foreign to us today and has been attacked with special vehemence by modern writers such as Kate Millett. In a powerful book entitled *Sexual Politics* she argued that the traditional family exploits and downgrades women while men in the home dominate everyone else like spike-helmeted Prussian tyrants.[2]

Probably none of us longs for a return to Victorian aloofness in the family, but sometimes we must wonder if the changes are coming too quickly. Within the past hundred years,

—family size has become smaller. This creates less confusion in the home, but there are fewer older children to help with the younger.
—family ties have becomer looser. Family members who work do so away from home. Entertainment has been taken over by the media, religious instruction has been taken over by the church, and education (including sex education) has been taken over by the schools, all of which strips the family of its closeness and many of its reasons for existing.
—family members have become scattered. Ours is an age of mobility, in which family members move frequently and often live hundreds of miles from the old family homestead. The result is lessened family support and companionship, and a turning to neighbors (instead of family) for fellowship and help in times of crisis.
—family roles have become fuzzier. There no longer appear to be clearly defined roles for the male or female

in the family. Often, both have careers and share in homemaking responsibilities. With the rise in divorce, there are an increasing number of families in which one adult takes over as both father and mother. All of this can be confusing to the children, who look for adult guidance in learning how to be a man or woman.

—family living styles have become less traditional. Marriage without children is becoming the chosen lifestyle for many couples. Others have chosen communes (with or without free sex), where children are raised by a group of couples who live and work together. Homosexual marriages are openly announced and increasingly accepted.

In light of these changes, we might ask if the family can maintain a semblance of stability while the whole institution of marriage is undergoing reexamination and transformation. Can we cope with stresses inside and outside the family and still maintain our sense of togetherness? Can family life survive when more and more people are settling for "trial marriages," mate-swapping, group marriages, or homosexual unions? Must we agree with Alvin Toffler[3] that, since conventional marriage is less and less capable of giving lifelong love, we must settle for a series of temporary marriages in which couples enter matrimony knowing that the relationship is likely to be short-lived?

I, for one, am not all that pessimistic. Certainly marriages and families are changing, but many of these changes are good. They are needed to keep us abreast of the twentieth century, but regretfully they are also accompanied by values which threaten not only the family but the whole of society. Self-centered individualism, the demand for freedom, belief in the superiority of pleasure— these are the attitudes which undermine the family. It is possible to counteract these influences, however, and the place to start is by facing head-on the stresses that we meet in our own homes.

REDUCING FAMILY STRESS

One of my students grew up in a family where the father was an alcoholic. At first the wife and children tried to ignore the problem, hoping it would go away, but the drinking got worse. Slowly, in embarrassment, the family began to withdraw from other people while the mother and older children took over many of the father's responsibilities.

In the years which followed, the father would periodically stop drinking and try to resume his place in the family. But when that happened, the mother would get depressed and difficult to endure in the home. Before long, in utter frustration, the father would return to the bottle and the mother would return to normal—taking over her family duties again but all the while complaining about her drinking spouse.

In this family it is easy to see how the actions of one person influence everyone else. Consider what happens when a couple gets married. Each person comes with habits, ideas, attitudes, opinions, beliefs, and ways of looking at life which have built up over many years. If marriage is to be successful, these parts of the personality must somehow be fitted together. During the excitement of dating, differences might not have been noticed, but in the reality of living together the conflicting aspects of two personalities seem to become apparent. This is stress which must be worked out by discussion or perhaps by trial and error.

Now let us assume that the couple works out a smooth relationship, but then the wife gets pregnant. All of a sudden a third person enters the scene. The marriage must adapt to new economic stresses, different demands on one's time, and perhaps an interference with the couple's vocational or social life. In one study, 83 percent of the couples interviewed reported that the first child's coming brought "extensive" or "severe" stress, even though in almost all cases the pregnancy was planned and the child was wanted.[4]

Whenever there is a change in the family, there must be a readjustment by everyone. A move to a new house, another child, a new pet, a business failure, your daughter's first day in school, your son's arrest, an injury or death of a family member, alcoholism in the home, the marriage of a child, retirement from a job—all of these, even the pleasant events, put stress on the family, and everyone must work at bringing stability out of the disruption. Since things like this go on all the time, there is almost always some stress in the home. The stress is more easily handled, however, if we keep several basic ideas in mind.

THE BIBLE AND MARRIAGE

First, we need to return to the Bible and build on God's plan for marriage and family stability. This is most explicitly stated in Ephesians chapters 5 and 6, where, in the middle of a discussion about the Christian life, we have a long reference to the family. Clearly, good Christian living and good family living are meant to go together.

Submission and Equality

Let's begin, like the Bible does, with God's plan for the wife and mother. She has a responsibility to submit to her husband as she would submit to Christ, and she should respect her mate.

As we are all aware, neither of these ideas has much popularity today, especially among advocates of women's liberation. Many have simply dismissed this advice as the bias of a male chauvinist, or have tried to explain it away so that "submission" means something other than submission. Both of these reactions create problems.

If we decide that the Apostle Paul's words are wrong, we have placed ourselves in the position of judging what is true in the Bible and what isn't, and the Bible is no longer our authority. *We* have become the authorities instead, and each of us decides what is right or wrong. The result can be chaos.

On the other hand, if we accept the Bible but interpret its words to mean that the wife is *not* to submit to her husband, we must be consistent in our reasoning and agree that Christians should not submit to Christ either! In the Bible the two ideas are tied together: "As the church is subject to Christ, so also the wives ought to be to their husbands in everything."[5] If one of these is true, so must be the other.

Part of the problem with this command for the wife's submission is our tendency to assume that submission implies inferiority. But in no place does the Bible imply that women are inferior to men. God has set up a system of authority which puts responsibility for family life on the male. This frees the wife to develop her greatest potential while the husband protects her from physical and other dangers. The husband and wife are equals. They even submit to each other,[6] but the wife realizes that ultimately the husband is head of the home.

Larry Christenson, a Lutheran pastor from California, has written about this in his popular book, *The Christian Family*.

> . . . it is important to distinguish between submissiveness and servility. A wife who sees that her husband's judgment is wrong or unwise should tell him so—with all respect, but freely and honestly. The judgment, wisdom, and opinion of a loving wife is one of a man's greatest assets. . . . A wife can be a person of strong, even outspoken opinions, and still be submissive to her husband's authority, if deep down she respects him and is quite prepared and content for him to make and carry out the final decision. . . .
>
> Thus, the subordinate role of the wife does not stifle her personality. On the contrary, it provides the best environment for her creativity and individuality to express itself in a wholesome way. It is God's way of drawing upon her gifts of intelligence, insight, and judgment, without at the same time burdening her with the authority and responsibility of [unnecessary] decisions. . . .

God has assigned a certain role in marriage to each partner. These respective roles are a part of the basic nature of marriage. To ignore them, or devise our own substitutes, is to invite a marital crack-up.[7]

Leadership

Turning to the husband, we see that his job is to take leadership responsibility in the home. According to the Bible, the man *is* head of the wife and family. He need not prove that he can, should, might, or could be responsible for the family. He is head of the home as Christ *is* head of the church.

Here again we may have visions of husbands cracking the whip and telling everyone else to shape up. That's not the Biblical picture. Christ showed His true greatness by being a humble servant—obedient to God, loving, and sensitive to the needs of mankind. This is exactly what is meant by headship. The husband takes responsibility for his family by loving and providing for them.

Love is a very confusing word in our society, for it is often equated with sex and nothing more. In the Bible, however, the husband is given a clear indication of what love means. First, love involves a caring willingness to give everything to the other person. That is how Christ loved the church. Second, husbands are to love their wives like they love their own bodies. A paraphrase of the golden rule for husbands could be, "Love you wife and do for her as you would like others to do for you." Husbands love by nourishing, cherishing, and providing for their wives.

On a TV talk show one time, a Latin American movie actor was asked a challenging question: "We know Latins are great lovers, and you have the reputation of a great screen lover. Now tell us, what makes a great lover?"

You can imagine the interest as the audience waited for some off-color remark about sex, but the reply was different: "A great lover is someone who can satisfy a woman all his life long, and be satisfied by one woman all his life long. A great lover is not someone who goes from woman to woman. Any dog can do that!"[8]

What About the Children?

Not long ago we were having a discussion in our family about the role of husbands and wives in the home. Soon one of my daughters sighed and asked, "How come we're talking so much about parents? What about the children?" I'm not sure my answer was appreciated by my daughter, because the Biblical instructions are pretty concise: "Children, obey your parents in the Lord, for this is right. Honor your father and mother."[9] Here again is the idea of submitting to parents and treating them with courtesy, kindness, and honor.

I can almost hear the parental cries of despair at this idea. "I can't even find the kids half the time. How do I teach submission, courtesy, kindness, and honor when my kids have never heard these words and spend so much time glued to the TV screen that we hardly have time to talk?" Clearly children are not innately disposed to obey and honor their parents. We must help them to do so by following the Biblical guidelines for being a good parent.

THE BIBLE AND PARENTS

A friend of mine recently faced the dilemma of deciding what to say to a group of teenagers to whom he had been invited to speak. After considerable time in preparation, he rehearsed his speech at the dinner table and got absolutely no response from the family. Finally his teenage daughter made a comment: "That's a nice speech Dad, but I'd throw it away. Why don't you tell them to be patient with their parents. After all, this is the parents' first time at raising a family, and they're not really sure what they're doing!"

My friend took the suggestion and wrote a new speech, which apparently was well received. His daughter's words were insightful. Isn't it amazing that God should entrust something as important as child-rearing into the hands of amateurs!

Once again, however, God has given us guidelines. First, *parents* must learn to obey. The idea of obedience comes up again and again in the Bible. Before asking, "How do my kids learn to obey their parents?" it would be good to ask, "How well do *I* obey my heavenly Father?" Rebellious parents have rebellious children. Children who see parental obedience have a model for doing likewise.[10]

Loving God and the Kids

A second guideline for parents is that we should not "provoke our children to anger," exasperating them so they lose heart.[11] If ever a Bible verse could be misinterpreted it is this one, especially when the misinterpretation comes from the lips of a ten-year-old!

According to Greek scholar Kenneth Wuest, the idea here is *not* that we should refrain from saying or doing anything that will upset our children. Instead, we parents should not be unjust and overly severe. It is easy to criticize children but to never encourage; to shout, but never to listen; to make demands, but never to explain why. Children are people too. They are entitled to respect and kindness—or to put it another way, they should be loved.

In one of His talks with the disciples, Jesus stated that love is the most outstanding characteristic of the follower of Christ.[12] When we love God, His love flows back through us and into others, including the people in our homes. This does not mean that we never correct our children. On the contrary, even God disciplines His children[13] and expects us to do likewise, but our discipline must be in love. Do you ever ask God to help you correct your children in ways that He would approve? God hears and answers such prayers.

Daring to Discipline

Discipline is not a popular idea, but neither is it optional for a parent. The Bible tells us to discipline our children. Do you remember old Eli? He was a priest in the Jewish temple, but he was so busy with his religious duties that he let his sons run wild, and this led to incredible family problems and grief.

But it isn't easy to discipline children effectively. How do we do it? According to Dr. James C. Dobson in his popular book, *Dare to Discipline*,

> A parent can absolutely destroy a child through the application of harsh, oppressive, whimsical, unloving and /or capricious punishment. . . . However, you cannot inflict permanent damage to a child if you follow this technique: identify the rules well in advance; let there be no doubt what is and is not acceptable behavior; when the child cold-bloodedly chooses . . . to challenge those known boundaries in a haughty manner, give him good reason to regret it; at all times, demonstrate love and affection and kindness and understanding. *Discipline and love are not antithetical*; one is a function of the other. The parent must convince himself that discipline (as outlined above) is not something he does *to* the child; it is something he does *for* the child. His attitude towards his disobedient youngster is this: "I love you too much to let you behave like that."[14]

Learning to Teach

The chief purpose of discipline is to teach appropriate behavior, but one need not be a professional educator to realize that teaching takes place in a variety of ways.

We teach by example. The late Mahatma Gandhi was once asked by a newspaper reporter if he could summarize his message in a few words. The old man thought a minute and then replied, "My life is my message."

Sometimes we confuse our children by giving double messages. "Always be honest," we say, and then we tell a neighbor something that isn't exactly true. At first this confuses children, but eventually they learn to follow what we do more than what we say. In child-rearing, our actions speak louder than our words.

We teach by instruction. Of course words are important. Old Testament parents were instructed to begin teaching early and to always be ready to discuss matters that came up. In our house, some of our greatest theological discussions have come up at the most unexpected times. The same has been true of our talks about sex. It is fine to have times set aside for teaching, but these should not replace those casual discussions that arise, for example, after observing some vandalism, seeing a movie advertisement, or hearing some misunderstood lyrics on the radio.

We teach by atmosphere. Perhaps this is the least explicit, but children pick up a lot just by being around us. How is your home decorated? What kind of a car do you drive? What type of music plays in your house? What do you watch on television? What does the family talk about at dinner? What are your Christmas cards like? All of this creates an atmosphere which teaches values and can have a tremendous impact on the growing child.

Taking Care of Needs

Parents have one more responsibility—to provide for their children. Naturally this brings thoughts of food, clothing, and shelter, but that's the easy part. Children also need attention from parents, the opportunity to talk, and times away from other activities. These are crucially important for a happy home.

FAMILY COMMUNICATION

If there is one major problem underlying all marital and family stress, it is this: communication has broken down. I suspect that in every book written about marriage (and there are hundreds of them), the importance of communication is emphasized at some point.

Good communication occurs when the communicator expresses what he or she really thinks or feels, and when the receiver picks up the message which was actually sent. Very often, however, this process gets garbled or hindered in some way, so that we don't know what the other person *really* means. At times we fail to say what we are thinking, or we refuse to listen, or we use words to hurt rather than to inform. All of this creates tension, which hinders real understanding. Because we have learned to be dishonest (usually by keeping quiet in the interests of politeness of diplomacy) we find it hard to speak the truth in love at home.

When we are frustrated it is especially easy to use what Mark Lee has called "the dirty dozen"—words which hinder communication rather than help.[15] These are *inflammatory words*, which arouse anger; *withheld words*, which ought to have been spoken; *discouraging words*, which are meant to destroy confidence or "put down" another person; *gossipy words*, which demean (e.g., "You know what people think about women who dress like you!"); *angle words*, which take a sideswipe at the other person (e.g., *His* wife knows how to cook"); *laughing words*, which are said as a joke when none is intended (e.g., "Isn't it funny how your clothes are all shrinking!"); *question words*, which really accuse (e.g., "How stupid do you think I am?"); *contradictory words*, which habitually disagree with the other person; *repetitious words*, which "rub it in"; *profane words*, of the "four-letter" variety; *egotistical words*, like "I told you so"; and *pronoun words*, which depersonalize (e.g. "*She* goes *her* way and I go mine," rather than "We like to work on separate projects").

Avoiding loaded terms like this will keep down the explosions, but this can lead to silence, which is no better. In fact, silence might even be worse, since then we rely on nonverbal communication, which is more easily misinterpreted.

LEARNING TO COMMUNICATE

So how do we communicate? The following suggestions might be helpful.

Pick an appropriate time and place. Most desirable is a room where everyone feels comfortable and where interruptions are likely to be minimal. Try to avoid discussing touchy issues when everyone is tired or when someone is in a hurry. But don't let this be an excuse for never discussing touchy issues.

Say it straight! The Clinebells describe a wealthy lady who decided to have a book written about her family. Much to her horror she discovered that one of her grandfathers had been electrocuted in Sing Sing prison. The woman wanted this fact hidden, so the following statement appeared in the book: "One of her grandfathers occupied the chair of applied electricity in one of America's best-known institutions. He was very much attached to his position and literally died in the harness."[16] To be deceptive, secretive, or defensive like this doesn't help communication. It is better to be honest, but to say things in a loving way that respects the other person.

Be aware of yourself. Family communication involves deep sharing, and the more we try to understand ourselves and our feelings, the better we share.

Listen carefully. Try to really understand what is being communicated. Don't interrupt, and check to make sure you get the message correctly. Recognize that people communicate by actions as well as by words. This is especially true of children who have difficulty expressing themselves verbally. If someone in your family is unusually grouchy or noisy, ask yourself why. Is this behavior communicating something that hasn't been said by words?

Be sensitive to feelings—your own and those of others. A cartoon once showed a man saying to his wife as they left a counselor's office, "Now that we've learned to communicate, shut up!" This is clear, but not very sensitive to how the other person might feel!

Learn to communicate with warmth. "I care" messages do a lot to smooth ruffled feathers. A hug, a pat on the hand or back, a pat on the head—these can all say "I love you," and that needs to be said frequently.

TAKING THE FAMILY SERIOUSLY

"To expect a marriage to last indefinitely under modern conditions is to expect a lot," wrote one observer. "To ask love to last indefinitely is to expect even more. . . . Of course there will be some who, through luck, interpersonal skill and high intelligence, will find it possible to make long-lasting monogamous marriages work. Some will succeed, as they do today, in marrying for life and finding durable love and affection. But others will fail. . . ."

This isn't a very optimistic view of marriage and family stability, but it may be a realistic picture of what is happening in our society. Might it be, however, that some people have given up, concluding that family stability and lifelong marital happiness is almost impossible? This is almost certain to bring disaster. If we don't resolve to make our families work, where is our hope for stability?

It's not easy to cope with marital stress. No two people are the same. We consist of different personalities which must be blended over a period of time. As we grow older our interests, needs, and aspirations change—and so should our marriages. All of this requires time, energy, work, sensitivity, and creativity, spiced with a willingness to try new approaches and a little humor so you can see the amusing side to life.

Paul Tournier tells of a brilliant and successful surgeon who was so caught up in his work that he almost ignored his wife completely.[17] When she began to get nervous symptoms he sent her to a psychiatrist, who told the husband to spend more time with his wife. Dutifully, the doctor began a ritual of taking his wife to a movie on Friday night, but he couldn't understand why she didn't get better.

Here was a couple, living in the same house, sharing the same bed, and not hurting each other, but strangers because they had let themselves drift apart. Somehow they had concluded that sitting side-by-side in a movie would make things better.

It takes courage to share your inner feelings with

another person, but it is absolutely essential for real personal growth and reduction of stress. I saw this in our house just a few days ago.

All of a sudden and without apparent reason one of our children seemed unhappy with everyone. She sulked at dinner, sassed her mother, tried to start an argument with her sister, and generally appeared to be mad at the world. Shortly after dinner, when the children were outside, our grouchy little daughter took a swing at one of the neighbor kids.

It was time for action, so father, excusing himself from the dinner guests, went marching out to take charge of the situation. Something inside told me to take it easy, however, so I gently pulled my daughter over to sit next to me on the step. "What's wrong with you tonight?" I asked, and immediately she began to talk about the troubles of being a nine-year-old. It was a beautiful experience as we shared together for half-an-hour, talking about the stresses of life. And the talk changed the whole atmosphere in our house that night.

The family can be our greatest source of stress, but it can also be a shelter in a world of stress and a stable schoolroom where all its members learn firsthand how to cope successfully with the pressures of life.

Chapter 7
SEXUAL STRESS

As I pulled up to the stoplight my eye caught the words on the bumper sticker ahead. "Remember," it asked, "when the air was clean and sex was dirty?"

At first I was amused, but then I began to ponder how things have changed in the last half-century. Around the time of the First World War a pious Dutch woman had written some advice for young people:

> Do not imagine that sexual life in marriage is anything very beautiful or pleasurable. It is a trick of Satan to tempt unmarried people to commit acts that God allows only married people to do, and then only so the human race might continue. . . . Nothing is more foolish than to enchant anyone with the notion that married relations are something very beautiful. There are thousands of things that are far nicer. A brisk walk, a fine bike ride, a visit to a museum, listening to good music: these are things that stay with us. The other is a moment, that can leave us revolted afterward.[1]

Think how foreign this seems to the world in which we live—a world where premarital sex is the norm rather than the exception; where seduction, nudity, and explicit sexual behavior are all accepted parts of theatrical performance; where topless waitresses, mate-swapping, gay sex, and abortion-on-demand have become part of our way of life; where pornographic books and magazines are openly displayed even in the racks of the "family drugstore"; where standards of right and wrong seem to have disintegrated; and where thousands of people, especially young people, wander in and out of promiscuous sexual relationships guided only by the common moral code of our era: "If it feels good—do it!"

Within just a few decades, sex has skyrocketed from a subject mentioned only in hushed tones (if at all) to something approaching a national public obsession. I remember the first time I visited England, back in the 1950's. I'm sure there were pornographic movie houses and bookstores even then, and that everyone knew about the prostitutes in the Soho district of London. But sex was, shall we say, kept under cover. Things were done in the English way: prim and proper. How different when I returned thirteen years later! Explicit references to sex seemed to be everywhere, and even the stuffy *Sunday Times* carried an advertisement section on men's fashions showing fully clothed males and completely unclothed women. References to sex seemed to be everywhere. A few months later, when I returned to North America, it became clear that the same change in sexual attitudes had been happening here, but I just hadn't noticed.

This is how revolutions always work. At first the change is gradual and hardly noticed; then comes a sudden break with the past and the sweeping introduction of a dramatic new situation.[2] The so-called sexual revolution has happened, whether we've noticed it or not. Things are different now from what they were 25 years ago. Our attitudes, expectations, and standards have all changed. And millions of people are in a state of aftershock, wondering, "What happened? How did we get here?" Suddenly we are faced with the overwhelming stress of adjusting to the new open view of sexuality which has become part of our society.

HOW DO WE RESPOND?

Revolutions can only be ignored for a short time. If we are to cope with stress successfully, we cannot and must not overlook the sexual changes that have been taking place within recent years. We *cannot* overlook the changes because they are so widespread and influential. In 1948, the *New York Times* refused to carry a medical textbook company's advertisement for the first Kinsey report. Twenty years later, without apparent reluctance, the *Times* was carrying almost-pornographic ads for books and movies that previously would have been banned as indecent.[3] Now we use sex to entertain, break up marriages, destroy feelings of self-worth, and sell everything from children's clothes and newspapers to kitchen tables and condominiums. The most intimate details of sexual behavior are now discussed openly, and even the most prudish among us are no longer shocked or surprised by the sexual looseness all around. In our unguarded moments of reflection it is easy to lean back and think: "These changes aren't so bad after all, so why fight them?"

That is why we *must not* ignore the changes. The rigid inhibitions of the early twentieth century undoubtedly created a lot of stress, to say nothing of guilt and phoniness, but we have gone too far the other way. We have accepted as normal and moral many behaviors which the Bible describes as sinful. We have taken what was intended for the privacy of marriage and have made it public. With our loose attitudes toward sex we are committing social suicide, according to a highly provocative but widely influential book by George Gilder. "Sex can be cheapened," Gilder writes, "but then, inevitably it becomes extremely costly to the society as a whole. For sex is the life force—and cohesive impulse—of a people, and their very character will be deeply affected by how sexuality is managed, sublimated, expressed, denied, and propagated. When sex is devalued, propagandized, and deformed, as at present, the quality of our lives declines and our social fabric deteriorates."[4]

SEX IS GOD'S IDEA

With all this concern over the abuse of sex, it is important not to lose sight of the fact that sex is God's idea. He made us male and female rather than unisexual. He gave us hormones, genitals, and the ability to fantasize. Surely He knew that this would put us under stress, but He also wanted us to experience the real joy of sex. So He gave us the impulses and bodies which could copulate, as well as the guidelines for self-control and maximum sexual satisfaction.

In a university class several years ago, a friend of mine read from the Song of Solomon and asked the class to guess the origin of what they had heard. "It came from *Playboy*," suggested one. "I think it's from a novel," said another. Everyone was surprised to learn that the Bible is explicit about sex. There is no reason to deny sex—that just creates stress. The first step in dealing with sexual stresses, however, is to recognize that sex was created by God.

THE PURPOSE OF SEX

Next, we need to consider the reasons why sex was created. The most obvious answer is that sex is for *reproduction*. After creating a male and female,[5] God's first commandment to the human race concerned sex. "Be fruitful and multiply," He said, "and fill the earth."[6] In the lush seclusion of the Garden of Eden, Adam and Eve may have quickly turned to obey. If so, that would have been quite consistent with the divine plan.

But sex was intended as more than a means of reproduction. Surely God would not have agreed with the lady whose advice was quoted earlier: that sexual intercourse is "only so the human race might continue." Sex is also God's way of enabling us to express *intimacy*. When a husband and wife "become one flesh"[7] there should be an interlocking of their bodies and minds in a tender and explosive ecstacy which leaves them relaxed and unified. Sex was intended by God to become a deep experience of physical, spiritual, and psychological pleasure between male and female.

There is a third purpose for sex: *enjoyment*. Just because the society has abused sex is no reason for concluding that sex is no fun. In the words of one writer, we should "rejoice and be glad in it."[8] The Old Testament tells the young husband to "rejoice" with his wife by letting "her breasts satisfy you at all times" and being "exhilarated always with her love."[9] Clearly sex is meant to be pleasurable.

Fourth, sex is for *the satisfaction of needs*. Paul the Apostle wrote that there may be value at times for a couple to abstain from intercourse, but that this should be only temporary. The husband and wife each have sexual needs which should be met by the other party.[10]

In their book *The Act of Marriage*, Tim and Beverly LaHaye suggest what lovemaking means to men and women. For the man, they write, intercourse satisfies the sex drive, boosts his sense of manhood, enhances his love for his wife, reduces friction at home, and provides life's most exciting experience. For the woman, sex fulfills her sense of womanhood, reassures her that she is loved, satisfies her sex drive, relaxes her nervous system, and provides the ultimately satisfying life experience.[11] When there are problems, sex doesn't always meet these needs adequately, but when intercourse is as God intended it to be, sex is entirely gratifying.

SEX AND MARRIAGE

What does this say to people who are not married? Have they been created with needs which can never be met? Must they live in lifelong stress if they cannot experience the intimacy and ecstasy that can come with sexual intercourse?

It is clear in the Bible that God intended sexual intercourse to be limited to married people. In the Scripture references which we have discussed so far, sexual intercourse is always assumed to take place between a husband and wife; this is the Biblical norm. Intercourse binds a couple into "one flesh," and this is true even if a man sleeps with a prostitute.[12] The Bible gives no grounds for promiscuity, mate-swapping, premarital sex, or extramarital affairs.

Does this imply that sexual fulfillment can come only to those who have a good sexual adjustment within marriage? What about the hundreds of thousands of persons who never marry? What about widows and widowers, the separated and divorced, and the couples who live together peacefully but without a truly satisfying sexual relationship? To say that these people are incomplete or perpetually frustrated is to misinterpret the real meaning of sex.

Sex involves much more than the penetration of a penis into a vagina. Admittedly, this can be the ultimate sexual experience, but human sexuality is far broader than a physical act. Indeed, this physical act of intercourse is sometimes nothing other than a momentary physical sensation followed by a cold emptiness. Sexuality is meant to be more than that!

Sexuality, as we have seen, involves *intimacy*. It involves a warm, trusting companionship with another person, a relationship of closeness, communion, and caring. Sexuality also involves *insight*. It lets us explore the mystery of another person and in turn be understood and accepted by another. In addition, sexuality involves *identity*. The questions of "Who am I?" or "What is my purpose in life?" very frequently center around questions of what it means to be male and how that differs from being female. Sexuality, therefore, is far more than intercourse, important as that may be. Whenever we relate to other people intimately we are relating as sexual creatures, and this need not lead to the bedroom.

As a human, Jesus was a sexually fulfilled person. He never had intercourse, but He was secure in His intimacy with others, His insight into Himself, and His personal identity. Paul was the same way. He didn't oppose marriage, as some people assume. He was in favor of it and taught clearly that for some people, especially those whose sexual urges were strong, it was better to marry than to burn with the stresses of unsatisfied sexual urges. But the Scriptures are clear in their demonstration that while sexual intercourse is limited to marriage, fulfillment as sexual beings can come to all of us, married and single alike.

SEX AND THE CHRISTIAN LIFESTYLE

From what has been said so far, it should come as no surprise that sex is quite consistent with holy living. Too often we forget this. Many people still have the idea that sex is something they must tolerate. Down deep they see it as a tool of the Devil, as some lecherous trait inherited from the fall of man, or as some annoying physical impulse that distracts us from the real Christian goal of obeying God and growing spiritually.

It is true that Satan often uses sex to tempt us, probably because for most of us this is where we are weakest and most vulnerable to sin. We must not forget, however, that sex is *God's* idea. He created us as sexual creatures, and He wants us to enjoy our sexuality.

Perhaps this is seen most clearly in Paul's First Letter to the Corinthian church. Corinth was a thoroughly corrupt society, in which people pretty well did what they felt like sexually. "If it feels good—do it!" could well have been a bumper sticker on their chariots, because this was the prevailing sexual norm. Paul therefore tries to give practical help to these Corinthian Christians. In the midst of a discussion of spiritual behavior, worship, and theology Paul inserts some of the New Testament's most explicit statements about sex.[13] "Glorify God in your body," we read, by meeting each other's sexual needs. It didn't seem strange to Paul that sex and personal holiness could go together. They are both part of the divine plan for mankind.

THE ABUSE AND MISUSE OF SEX

It doesn't take a theologian or psychologist to realize that this divine plan is frequently ignored by most contemporary people. Promiscuity, gay relationships, bisexuality, and a host of other sexual lifestyles have become widely accepted. In contrast, the Bible warns against sexual sin and condemns fornication (sex before marriage), adultery (sex outside marriage), homosexuality, and other forms of immorality.[14]

In a book written to help people cope with stress, I certainly do not want to raise the stress level of my readers. There is real danger of this when we begin to point out that God will judge us for sexual sins. Most of us are guilty—and the guilt feelings hardly need to be accentuated with Biblical accounts of judgment.

But God's judgment must always be seen in the light of divine mercy and help. God cannot tolerate sin. He is holy and completely fair. There can be no bribes to pay Him off, no successful attempts to have the rules changed. God's standards are clear, explicit, and unalterable. This gives us a sense of security in that we know exactly where we stand. Along with this, however, is clear Biblical teaching about forgiveness. If we confess our sins—really feel sorry for what we have done and ask forgiveness, God forgives—just like that![15] And there is something else. God gives us the ability to control our sexual impulses and bring them into line with His standards. That news isn't stress-producing. It's liberating. It can free us from compulsions, release us from guilt and guilt feelings, liberate us from the manmade rules about sex which cause so much confusion, and free us from the illusion that orgasm is the source of all fulfillment and joy.

CONTROLLING SEXUAL STRESSES

What is your major problem in life? I asked this of a large group of students recently, and you might guess what kind of answer came back. Well over half the students wrote that their number one problem was an inability to control themselves, especially in the area of sex.

Two Fallacies

The place to start with self-control is to get rid of two common fallacies. Frequently accepted without question, these two faulty conclusions do much to keep us under continual sexual stress. The first fallacy is this: "I'm the only one!" Do you have lustful thoughts? Is sexual control a problem for you? Have you struggled with masturbation? If so, join the crowd. These things are very common. This doesn't make them right, but it helps us to realize that other people are struggling with the same pressures. In fact, it is probable that your personal pressures are a lot more common than you think.[16]

The second fallacy is, "I will never change!" In all compassion and gentleness let me state that this is nonsense. If God is all-powerful (even more than the Devil who tempts us), then change is always possible. The Christian has no justification for a loss of hope.[17]

Coming to grips with these ideas may take time. These fallacies are so prevalent and so ingrained that they are not cast off overnight. In throwing these off, you might jettison a few others: "I'm dirty," "I'm a freak," "I'm oversexed," "I must be very immature," "God will never use someone as bad as me." All of these keep us under stress, and none of these is likely to be true.

Confession

This gets us to the next step in self-control: confession to God. This involves a prayerful attitude, telling God what we have done, telling Him we are sorry and want to change (if we aren't really repentant and don't want to change, tell God about that too and ask Him to give you these desires), and asking Him to cleanse us and to give us the power to overcome the problem. God answers prayers like these because they are clearly in His will and because He has promised to answer.[18]

Sometimes there can be real value in confessing to someone else and asking for encouragement, support, and prayer. This is clearly taught in the Bible[19] and has been proven conclusively by Alcoholics Anonymous. Here is a group of people who are open enough to confess their problems, concerned about helping one another, and inclined to pray together. Be careful to whom you confess, however. Confession can be risky, especially if your confessor can't keep a secret. But confession to someone can also help you with self-control.

Other Ways to Go

Is there some other, more acceptable way to channel off your anxieties? When the problem is one of anger or nervous tension, it is often helpful to play tennis, work out in a gym, or find a relaxing hobby. It is more difficult, however, when the tension is sexual. Books are filled with advice about taking cold showers, jogging, or otherwise distracting yourself when you are sexually aroused. Remember, however, that God made us sexual, and hundreds of cold showers won't wash that away.

Nevertheless, there is some merit in diversionary activity. When we are busy, enjoying sports, or involved in creative activities and close interactions with other people, then we are less inclined to be introspective and not so likely to be concentrating on our struggles with self-control. In the words of one respected scholar, "The real cure for evil thoughts is good action."[20]

It is certain that we do not get rid of stressful thoughts or sexual temptations by deciding not to think about them. "I'm not going to think about sex today" is a good way of concentrating your mind on the very things you wish to forget. It makes better sense to fill your mind with good thoughts. Psychologists tend to avoid the "mind," but this is a word used again and again in the Bible: we are to have a mind like Christ, to think about godly things and to focus our attention on that which is pure, lovely, praiseworthy, and excellent.[21] The mind has been called the biggest sex organ in the body. Many of our sexual stresses start there, and it is there that they are most effectively attacked.

Avoiding the Danger Areas

I have a friend who is an alcoholic. When we discussed his problem recently he told me how he likes to have lunch in a little café near his office. Regretfully, they serve liquor there and sometimes my friend never gets up from the table until well into the evening. One thing this man must learn is to avoid eating in places which serve alcohol. He can't resist the temptation.

The same applies to the realm of sex. Since we live in a society which parades physical sex, it is difficult if not impossible to avoid temptations which are intended to "turn us on"—temptations that appear in newspaper ads, television, plays, and elsewhere. If we have problems in this area, however, the stresses are only accentuated by reading pornographic novels and magazines, attending erotic movies, or listening to sexually stimulating music.

Solo Sex

Nowhere does all of this apply more strongly than with the problem of masturbation, the deliberate stimulating of one's own genitals, usually to the point of orgasm.

In my library I have a book which claims authoritatively that masturbation ruins our health, develops introversion, forces us to withdraw into a world of fantasy, causes us to be horders, and generally creates an unhappy life. If all of this were true, a lot of people would be in pretty bad shape! The fact is, however, that masturbation is very common, it does not indicate mental instability or perversion, and it does not affect us physically. It is probably the most common sexual activity. Almost everyone does it or has done it, but we rarely discuss it.

Masturbation is a source of stress for many people. Unlike adultery, fornication, or homosexuality, masturbation isn't even mentioned in the Bible. Of course it is dangerous to argue from silence, but if masturbation were really harmful, wouldn't we expect to find something in the Bible about a stress which affects so many people?

I agree with Dr. David Seamands and others who conclude that the act of masturbation is in itself neither good nor evil.[22] It is clearly a second-best activity, but it can also be a temporary source of release for teenagers and college-age people (whose sex drives are especially active but who are not yet ready for the intimacy of marriage), for single people, or for those married persons who must refrain from intercourse because of events like a short-term separation or a spouse's illness.

The problem with masturbation is not so much with the act itself as with other related problems. First, there is *fantasy*. The Bible says nothing about masturbation but it does condemn lust. According to one study, three-fourths of all males fantasize during masturbation and so do about half of the females.[23] This could be classified as "mental adultery," and that is wrong.[24] Our minds must focus on that which is pure.

Second, there is a problem with *guilt*. How often do people masturbate, feel very guilty, and then decide that it will be a couple of weeks before they can get back into divine favor? That kind of thinking is unbiblical. If we masturbate, we should humbly confess our sinful thoughts, ask God to forgive us, and trust Him to help us forget it and control it.

Third, masturbation can become a *habit*. When this happens it masters us and sometimes becomes our major way of relieving tension. As Christians we must not be mastered by anything or anyone other than Christ.[25] Here again, confession and support from a fellow believer can help. Remember too that there are other, more effective ways to cope with tension.

Perhaps most serious is the problem of masturbation

becoming a *substitute* for deep interpersonal relations. Masturbation can be a "copout from the challenge of creating the personal closeness of partnership that is meant by intercourse, and hence may be an escape from one's partner."[26] The masturbator in this situation escapes from others by moving into the safer world of fantasy. No longer, then, does it seem necessary to build interpersonal relationships. No wonder that with married people there follows a decline in the joys of sex with one's mate.

Masturbation can sometimes be a peg on which we hang a lot of other problems. If the masturbation persists, especially as a compulsion into adulthood, we should discuss this with a friend or counselor who can help us see what might be at the basis of our stressful solo-sexual habit.

GETTING ALONG IN BED

I once had a friend who, prior to his marriage, read just about every sex manual he could get his hands on. "Did it help you?" I asked him a few years later (and a few weeks before my own wedding).

"Not much," he replied. "Some of the techniques were okay, but at times the books were contradictory, and we seemed to get along pretty well just 'doing what comes naturally.' "

For many people that is all they need. They need sensitivity to each other's needs, desire, patience, and a willingness to experiment with position and intercourse techniques. But it doesn't always work that way, and often "what comes naturally" is not very satisfying. Consider, for example, some of the common lovemaking problems that married couples encounter:

Embarrassment

This often comes at the beginning of marriage and may reflect a background which has emphasized modesty and/ or a fear of sex. One writer suggests that couples undress each other completely on the first night and explore each other's bodies.[27] This is not a bad idea, especially if done slowly and gently, although some couples may wish to start with an exploring by touch rather than by sight. With a sense of concern for each other, the embarrassment should quickly disappear.

Disappointment

We have grown accustomed to expecting every orgasm to be wildly exciting, but that doesn't always happen, especially at the beginning. The act of lovemaking is something we learn, and this takes time.

There are a number of suggestions for increasing sensitivity and overcoming the stress of disappointment. One of the simplest is to ask each other for feedback: "Does that feel good? Am I stimulating you in the right place?" It is also helpful to recognize that foreplay, the massage and fondling of each other's body prior to intercourse, takes times and should not be rushed. Remember that the woman takes a longer time to reach a state of arousal than does the man. He can reach an orgasm, ejaculate his semen, and roll over and go to sleep while a women is still becoming aroused. This, of course, leads to great frustration, especially in females. But this is a problem which could be avoided if couples would talk about their sensations and if husbands were a little more patient (trying, for example, to delay ejaculation temporarily by thinking about nonsexual things until the wife is more ready).

Inability to Attain Orgasm

There are, according to Dr. David Reuben,[28] literally millions of women who fail to reach an orgasm and, as a result, find sexual intercourse to be an emotionally stressful experience. Add to this the problem of impotence (when the male cannot get or maintain an erection) or premature ejaculation (when the ejaculation comes too soon, the penis goes limp, and the wife gets frustrated) and you have the basis of further stress in bed. Various studies have pointed out how ignorance of sexual anatomy, resentment and anger, guilt, fear of intercourse or of not being sexually responsive, fatigue, and a variety of other influences can prevent pleasurable orgasms. Regretfully, one or two failures builds fear of further failure, and this makes further failure almost inevitable.

These are major problems with many couples, but they are solvable problems. I would recommend that a couple with these and other sexual problems read Tim and Beverly LaHaye's *The Act of Marriage*.[29] Then, if problems persist, it would be good to seek a competent counselor.

What's Right?

Recently after speaking at a men's retreat, I heard a knock at my door and encountered a member of the audience, around thirty years of age. He wanted to know if it was "natural" for him and his wife to engage in oral-genital contacts. They both enjoyed it, but the wife wondered if it was really moral.

This is one of many questions about lovemaking which is not mentioned in the Bible. So long as it is not a substitute for intercourse, and so long as both partners feel comfortable in experimenting with various forms of sexual stimulation, it seems that we should say "anything goes."

SEX ON THE BRAIN

In our sex-dominated society, almost everyone at some time encounters sexual stresses of some sort. There are problems of self-control for married and single people alike, struggles with masturbation, tendencies toward homosexuality, the pain of unwanted pregnancies, the pressures to engage in sex outside marriage, the guilt over sexual sins, the concern over what is right and proper, the search for effective contraceptives, and the ethics of abortion, to name a few.

There is, in addition, the entire sex-related question of roles. How can I be a truly masculine male in our society today or a truly feminine woman? These questions have come into sharp focus within the past few years and they create stress in many lives, especially in young people. It is no longer necessary, it seems, for men and women to dress differently or to stick with clearly defined male and female jobs. Women, for example, now climb telephone poles while male telephone operators man the switchboards. This confusion over roles is stress-producing and is likely to remain so until, and if, we settle on some new and more clearly defined picture of what it really means to be male or female.[30]

The Subconscious

Many years ago, psychologists began to recognize that not everything in our mind is always conscious. There probably are memories, thoughts, and desires which exist at a subconscious level and influence our actions even without our awareness of what is happening.

I wonder if this has an influence on our sexual behavior. I once read an article in which the author discussed David's sexual sin with Bathsheba.

Do you remember the story? David's troops were at war and the king's concern kept him awake. During the night he slipped out onto the roof for some fresh air and saw Bathsheba taking a bath. Soon the king had her brought to the palace, they had intercourse, and Bathsheba got pregnant. This, of course, was embarrassing because Bathsheba's husband, Uriah, was at war with the troops.

David ordered Uriah home and encouraged him to sleep with his wife. But the man refused. His fellow soldiers didn't have that privilege, he replied, so why should he? This led David to plot Uriah's death.

Why, we might wonder, would an otherwise godly

man like David stoop to such tactics? Why was he, a married man, so overwhelmed with passion for a neighbor's wife that he got her pregnant?

Could the answer be in David's subconscious mind? If he perpetually fed his mind with sexually immoral thoughts, when the opportunity to sin arose he responded quickly. David's sin with Bathsheba was wrong, but I wonder if it could have begun long before he spied the neighbor woman from the rooftop that night.

This is speculation, of course. David may have had a very moral thought life, but one which collapsed when he encountered a highly sensual temptation. Whether his thoughts were pure or not, however, it is still true that the mind is our biggest sex organ and the greatest source for sexual stress. Resentments, fears, and insecurities can all create sexual stress, but so can a perpetual dwelling on sex—a ruminating which makes us prime candidates for overt sexual behavior when the opportunity presents itself.

It's a simple answer, but perhaps the best advice for coping with sexual stress is that of the New Testament: whatever is true, honorable, right, pure, lovely, good, excellent, and praiseworthy, think on *these* things.[31]

Chapter 8
OCCUPATIONAL STRESS

Almost everybody has heard about brainwashing. It was big news during the Korean War, when the Communist Chinese tried to change the thinking of thousands of Western prisoners of war. The pattern usually began by getting the prisoners exhausted and malnourished. In this physically weakened condition the men in the prison camps were then indoctrinated—told about the superiority of Communism and the inferiority of other systems. Contact with their families and with the rest of the world was cut off, meals and sleeping times became irregular, a spy system (sometimes more imagined than real) kept the prisoners in a state of fear or uncertainty, and at times all of this was accompanied by torture.

Some of the most interesting studies of brainwashing were done by a psychologist named Edgar Schein. Several years ago this same Dr. Schein made the surprising observation that in many business corporations something like brainwashing still goes on every day. The methods are less severe than in Korea, of course, and less emotional, but when young college graduates come to work they are sometimes subtly and slowly indoctrinated into the ways of the company. They are expected to commit themselves wholly to the company, their hours are demanding and irregular, promotion is uncertain, boredom is common, and they often get discouraged and frustrated. If the new employee fits, fine, but if not, he or she usually quits, often within a year or two of joining the firm. Within five years, roughly half of all the employees hired out of college have quit their jobs and moved elsewhere.[1]

I have a friend like that. We'll call him Frank. After graduating from high school, Frank went to work for a drug company. The pay was pretty good and so were the hours, but Frank was dissatisfied, so he quit and went back to school. But that wasn't very satisfying either. Without any goals there wasn't much motivation to study, so Frank took a job as a salesman and stuck it out for about a year. His life has continued like that for a long time. Now close to fifty, Frank works in a factory at a job which he hates. He had never intended to stay there for ten years. It had started off as a temporary position until something better came along, but when the family began to grow Frank decided to "stick it out for a while longer." Sometimes he thinks about changing again, but jobs are hard to get—especially for a man his age—and with teenagers going to school, he can't risk taking any position that would give a lower salary, fewer benefits, and less job security. So Frank goes to work every morning and counts the hours until quitting time. He's also looking forward to retirement. Only fifteen years to go!

THE STRESSES OF WORK

Apparently there are a lot of people like Frank. In fact, various surveys reveal that more than half of the people interviewed dislike their jobs. The reasons for this vary, and only part of the problem appears to stem from inadequate pay, poor working conditions, or lack of promotions.

Let's go back to those college graduates moving into the business world. When they were interviewed it was discovered that salary and fringe benefits didn't really make much difference. The new employees wanted *challenge*— an opportunity to test themselves to see if they could make a meaningful contribution to the company. They wanted to be treated with *respect*, as human beings, and not be viewed simply as young kids who are too ambitious, too immature, or too much interested in making money. They wanted *job satisfaction*, so that their work did not throw them into a rut of boredom. Many also hoped for *feedback*, some indication from the boss about how well they were doing. When these things were lacking, the young employees tended to lose their enthusiasm and to become apathetic, frustrated, and interested in finding another job.

Not everybody has so much freedom to move. Consider the housewife, for example. Many homemakers find their jobs to be creative and enjoyable, but others feel that the work brings no challenge, is unappreciated, is boring, and isn't even noticed (except when it isn't done). Work for such people is all stress and little fun. There isn't much time off and the housewife ends up with no pay and few fringe benefits.

Workaholics

But even when work is fun it can create stress. Several years ago Professor Wayne Oates electrified a lot of people with a book titled *Confessions of a Workaholic.*[2] The thing which made this book so disturbing (at least to me) was the writer's vivid description of a very common malady— involvement in work so complete that there was almost no time for vacations, for family, or for anything other than the job. The workaholic spends fifty to sixty hours a week or more at work, including most evenings. He or she has few hobbies, spends most "spare time" reading or thinking about the job, gets "antsy" when away from the office too long, and finds that there is never much time to relax or to do something other than one's work. This is a common problem of professional and business people, but it can hit any of us. Our work can become so satisfying and so demanding that it consumes us instead of being under our control.

Why Work?

When God created man, work appeared to be a part of the divine plan. Adam was instructed to cultivate the garden and to watch over it. In the beginning this work was probably very enjoyable, but after eating the forbidden fruit Adam found that his work got harder. With modern technology our work is probably less difficult today, but the ultimate reason for working has not changed. We work because God made us that way. Just as we cannot be totally fulfilled apart from Him, neither can we be completely fulfilled apart from work.

There are other reasons why people work, reasons which are less profound but more acceptable to the modern mind. Some work to survive, while others want to raise their standard of living.

It is also important to recognize that our jobs determine our place in society. The corporation president, for example, has more status and money than the man on the assembly line. Our work determines where we live, the friends we have, the kind of car we drive, the style of life we live, and, to some extent, even the churches where we worship. In addition, work can be a meaningful activity which stimulates us intellectually and gives us a sense of accomplishment and well-being. But, as we have seen, work also can be stressful, and few things are more frustrating than spending most of your life with people you don't like, doing something you don't enjoy.

STRESS AND THE DRIVE FOR SUCCESS

One of the major reasons for stress at work is the idea, ingrained in our thinking, that work is a measure of our self-worth. This is especially true of males. To justify our existence and prove to ourselves that we are valuable people, we assume that we must succeed on the job. If we don't succeed at work, so the myth goes, then maybe we aren't worth much as persons. So we start pushing to get ahead, hardly pausing to realize that when one person moves ahead, someone else gets pushed aside.

When I was in graduate school, we learned that it was important to be successful. It wasn't always stated ex-

plicitly, but the implication was that in order to be successful as psychologists we had to prove our worth by writing
articles or books, by achieving fame and status, and by
earning enough money so that we could live an obviously
affluent lifestyle. Since graduation I have watched many of
my colleagues push to be successful and to demonstrate all
these marks of vocational accomplishment. Too often,
however, broken marriages, ulcers, excessive drinking, and
discouragement have come along as by-products of this
great push to get ahead.

THE EXAMPLE OF PAUL TOURNIER

Probably all of us admire the person who "makes it"
and becomes successful in his job, but have you ever
thought what success really means? Several years ago I met
a man who is clearly successful, Dr. Paul Tournier, author
of seventeen books that have been highly acclaimed and
translated into eleven languages. Tournier is a famous man,
much in demand as a speaker, and extremely successful as a
counselor. He has had a successful marriage, has raised a
fine family, is well off financially, and lives in a very
modern home on the outskirts of Geneva, Switzerland.
When I first met Tournier, however, the thing that impressed me most was his sincere humility. He was clearly a
man who was interested in others more than in himself, and
he was not especially concerned about the worldwide
acclaim that for many years had come his way.

Following my visit to Geneva I decided that for me
success meant being something like Tournier: known
around the world, famous as an author, in demand as a
speaker, well off financially, able to integrate psychology
and theology, a superb teacher, a devoted husband, a proud
father, and one who influences thousands of lives for Christ.
As I looked at myself it became increasingly apparent that
these things not only represented success for me, but, like
many other people, I was pushing to be successful in accord-

ance with my own personal little plan. And I was working to build an empire—my own.

There is nothing wrong with wanting to succeed or to do well, but I still become uncomfortable and embarrassed when I look back over this list. If we are honest with ourselves, I think each of us could come up with a similar list of what represents personal success. We might not like the list, and yet we find ourselves pushing to attain the characteristics that are on that list. I see this driving for success at psychology conventions. I see it in my neighbors, in my professional colleagues, and in my students. Most distressing, I see it in myself, and I have come to realize that such a drive for success is not what God wants for each of our lives.

GOD'S STANDARD OF SUCCESS

If we search the Scriptures we see that God's standards for success are often very different from human standards. It is true that a man like Job, at least in the early part of his life, was successful both in God's eyes and in the opinion of men around him. But consider Jeremiah, John the Baptist, or even Jesus. These men were respected by God but rejected by the world. Christians, therefore, must strive to bring their definitions of success into line with what might be God's requirements of success for each one of us.

One of the most beautiful Biblical descriptions of success is found in Romans 12. In this familiar passage we see four characteristics of success from God's perspective.

Holiness

First, to be really successful in God's eyes our lives must be characterized by *holiness*. Romans 12:1 tells us, "I urge you therefore, brethren, by the mercies of God, to present your bodies a living and *holy* sacrifice acceptable to God." This is not a popular idea. We live in a time when getting ahead in one's work is considered far more important than living a holy life which is acceptable to God. It seems to me, however, that we could reach the height of success in terms of money, prestige, promotions, and acclaim; we could be successful leaders—even Christian leaders—but still be failures in God's sight because we neglect true holiness.

How can one live a holy life in our society? The clue to this comes in verse 2: "Do not be conformed to this world, but be transformed by the renewing of your mind." Part of the secret of holiness depends on what we do with our minds.

In his Letter to the Philippians the Apostle Paul urged his readers to let their minds dwell on things that are true, honorable, right, pure, lovely, of good repute, excellent, and worthy of praise.[3] To live successful and holy lives, therefore, our thoughts must be brought into conformity with the Bible's teachings, and that implies that our minds should be feasting on the Word of God. Too often we are so busy getting ahead with our work that there is no time for prayer, meditation, or thoughts about holy living. To be successful in God's eyes, we must be men and women whose lives are characterized by holiness.

Obedience

A second divine measure of success is *obedience*. The Christian is responsible for doing the will of God, that which is good and acceptable and perfect.[4] Psychologists sometimes talk of double messages. This occurs when we say one thing and mean something else. If we say to God, for example, "I'll do what you want me to do," but then add a few stipulations, we are really giving God a double message. We are saying in essence: "I have worked out my own plan and am coming to you for a divine rubber stamp of approval." This is not obedience. Obedience is conforming to God's will, not trying to bend God's will to fit ours.

When Joshua took over the difficult task of leading the children of Israel, the Lord spoke to him about success and defined this success in terms of obedience: "Be strong and very courageous. . . . Be careful to do according to all the law which Moses My servant commanded you; do not turn from it to the right or to the left, so that you may have success wherever you go. This book of the law shall not depart from your mouth, but you shall meditate on it day and night, so that you may be careful to do according to all that is written in it; for then you will make your way prosperous, and then you will have success" (Joshua 1:7, 8). Joshua clung to this. He attempted to obey God and he was clearly successful in the eyes of God.

Acceptance

Acceptance is a third divine characteristic of success. The term is easily misunderstood. Sometimes, for example, acceptance is used as an excuse for doing nothing. I once had a student who was flunking out of school but decided to accept this as the will of God. As a result he made no effort to improve his grades. This might be called laziness or neurosis, but it certainly was not acceptance. Acceptance, I believe, is recognizing that God has a place for us in the body of Christ. It may not be a place of preeminence, but it is a place consistent with the skills, abilities, opportunities, and gifts which God has given to each of us. In verses 3-5 of Romans 12 we discover that some of us are to be teachers, some are to be preachers, and some have other responsibilities, but we do not all serve in the same place doing the same things. I'm not a Paul Tournier, but neither is Paul Tournier a Gary Collins. God has given each of us different roles, different responsibilities, different places in the body of Christ, and different success in the world's eyes. My task is not to build myself up, to use other people in order to push myself ahead, or to struggle for fame. Instead, each of us has a responsibility to develop the skills and gifts that God has given us, to use our unique abilities for His service, and to accept with gratitude His place for us in the body of Christ.

Diligence

The fourth characteristic of success is *diligence*.[5] God expects us to do the best we can with the abilities we have and the opportunities that we are given.

Recently I spoke at a pastor's conference on the topic of stress and success in the ministry. During the course of our discussion one pastor described his frustrations at being in a small church in a rural community where he had seen almost no growth in the size of his congregation. The pastor was in his fifties, and I got the impression that he had worked very hard for many years in his parish. Sitting next to me in this discussion was another pastor, in his early thirties, whose church was the largest and fastest-growing congregation in the whole denomination. In the eyes of the world the young man was clearly more successful than the older man, but while we look on the outward appearance it is well to remember that God still looks on the heart. It may be that in His eyes these two pastors were equally successful, even though men would say that one had a more successful ministry. God measures success not by human acclaim, money, or status, but more in terms of the four standards of personal holiness, obedience, acceptance, and diligence on the part of His followers. With this more realistic definition of success, all of us can be successful, perhaps not in the eyes of the world, but in the eyes of God. That's where our real worth resides.

THE FEAR OF SUCCESS

All of this assumes, of course, that success is desirable—something which everyone wants and is striving to attain. In a recent book, however, psychiatrist Leon Tec argues that this isn't always so. Many people, he argues, have an inner fear of success.[6]

When we are successful, people expect more of us, and this can put us under terrific stress. It is safer and less demanding, therefore, to merely work in the factory than to be the boss, to be an average housekeeper instead of living with the reputation that you are "a fantastic hostess and gourmet cook," to be an average student instead of heading the class, to be a struggling author or a small-time athlete rather than a superstar. Superstars, like other successful people, have a reputation to maintain, and this can create a lot of anxiety. In addition, successful people are often criticized, sometimes unjustly, by those who are less successful and are envious of the one who has "made it." I am reminded of a very intelligent little girl I once knew who would fail a test periodically because it was too lonely and demanding to be considered the "class brain."

To be successful is satisfying and exciting, but it can also be risky and demanding. So how do we live with success? We recognize, first, that our successes come from God. Even when we think we have made it by our own efforts, we must remember that it is God who gave us the abilities, aspirations, and opportunities to get ahead. The successful man or woman has no reason to boast in his or her own achievements.[7]

But neither need we feel insecure in our success. Our value as persons is based neither on the continuous acclaim of others nor on their lack of praise for our efforts. Our value is based on the truth presented in the Bible that God loves us and finds us to be worthy creatures, regardless of our status in the world. Our task is to thank God for our successes or failures, to expect that He will meet our needs as He has promised,[8] and to pray that He will enable us to relax in our success and do the best we can, whether or not this meets the standards or expectations of somebody else.

Not long ago I was talking informally with a foreign student and suggested casually that if I could ever do anything to help him feel welcome, he should just let me know. A few weeks later I got a cable from London: "Arriving Thursday, 7 P.M. Please meet plane."

To put it mildly, I was indignant! This meant changing an appointment and driving 45 minutes to the airport. Didn't the student know that as a busy professor I had other things to do besides coping with traffic jams and jostling crowds at the airport? Then I remembered the words of Jesus, and my whole attitude changed: if you want to be great in life, really successful, be a servant.[9] That was what Jesus did, and everyone agrees that His work was successful and His life fulfilling. I was glad to meet my friend at the plane.

HANDLING OCCUPATIONAL STRESS

From all of this we might conclude that one way to cope with the problems of occupational stress is by looking at them from a different point of view. Think of success from God's perspective, for example, and you'll be less bothered by your success or lack of it as defined by others.

Very often, vocational problems come more from ourselves and from our own attitudes than from our working conditions. This can be true in any occupation. In a recent book on stress in corporation executives, the author began by stating that "the main source of psychological stress on the executive does *not* come from business problems."[10] It comes from how he manages his own feelings and the attitudes which are stirred up by the business. The man or woman at work may feel envy, anger, or discouragement in the job, but instead of coping with these inner feelings and getting a realistic perspective on the situation, he ignores his emotions.[11] As a result there is a reduction in production and efficiency and often an increase in alcoholism, family problems, and mental illness. In these situations the frustrated worker bolsters his or her waning self-confidence by drinking, and often the stresses of work are taken out on the family at home.

How can we handle this kind of stress? First, by taking a realistic look at the problem. What is it about your work that is making you unhappy? How is this affecting you? Is there anything you can do to make your work more meaningful, more interesting, less demanding, etc.?

Second, have a look at your attitudes. Is bitterness or cynicism making your job worse? Can you see anything positive in what you are doing? Have you ever thought that God may want you where you are? He doesn't put everyone in a leadership position. And remember that your place of work does not determine your worth as a person.

Third, beware of the myth of indispensability. No person is irreplaceable. Many of us remember the day President Kennedy was shot. One of the most important jobs in the world was suddenly vacated, but life went on without much interruption. It is sometimes difficult to accept the fact, but if we were killed tomorrow the world could get along fine without our labors, important though they seem today.

Fourth, make life as balanced and meaningful as you can. Your work is only a part of your life. It shouldn't be allowed to control everything you do, nor should it be permitted to drag you down into perpetual misery. Time with your family, hobbies, community activities, church work—all of these can bring balance to your life.

The problem comes when we don't have proper priorities. What is really most important for you right now? What goals do you have for your life and family? Where do you think God wants you to be? By jotting these things down on paper, you can get a better perspective on where you're going. Life can become more meaningful and less stressful when you find some satisfying purpose to replace what to this point may have been a frustrated drifting.

STRESS AND THE PROBLEM OF MONEY

It is difficult to talk about occupational stress without raising the issue of money. It is true that feelings of accomplishment, intellectual stimulation, and a sense of worth may all be part of our reason for working, but most of us look forward to payday with enthusiasm and necessity.

In itself money is only paper with little intrinsic value, but people run themselves ragged (sometimes with two or three jobs) trying to earn it, they enter innumerable contests trying to win it, they use credit cards to spend it before it comes in, they hoard it when they do have it, and they sometimes even steal it, either blatantly (like robbing a bank) or subtly (like cheating on income tax). The reason for all of this, of course, is that money represents something else. It lets us get the material things we want and it often lets us buy temporary psychological benefits, such as acclaim and attention (when we flaunt our money), self-esteem (when we give charitable gifts), relief from guilt (when, for example, we give money to the children that we feel guilty about rejecting), and sometimes friendship (the person with money often has at least a few greedy followers). In Western society, money means power, it brings status, and it is a mark of success. The person who drives an expensive car or lives in a big house is saying to the world, "I'm a successful person in a world which values success."

Money and the Bible

The Bible never condemns riches, nor does it imply that to be rich is wrong. We are warned against an overdependence on money, however, and we are told that the love of money can lead to all sorts of evil, even causing some to wander away from God.[12] Most of us have less money than we want, and our "itch for more" can be the source of innumerable stresses.

In His Sermon on the Mount, Jesus gave a number of practical guidelines for handling money in a way that would reduce our financially based stresses.[13]

Viewing Money Realistically

First, Jesus taught that earthly possessions, including money, are to be viewed realistically. Possessions, Jesus said, are *temporary*. Whether we own much or little, we could be wiped out tomorrow. If our peace of mind, status, self-esteem, and friendships are based on what we possess, we could quickly become as miserable and downtrodden as the prodigal son. Then, Jesus warned, possessions are *potentially harmful.* If they become too important they can distract us from God. We can't serve both God and money. In addition, possessions must be of *secondary importance.* We may not think so, but according to Jesus the building up of treasures on earth is far less important—and less secure— than building treasures in heaven. When we obey Him and seek His will in our lives we are storing up valuables in heaven, where there are no moths, no rust, and no thieves.

How do you respond when a valuable possession is lost or broken? This is a good measure of how you view your possessions. We have a responsibility to take care of what God has given us, but with God's help we must view our possessions realistically and avoid overattachment.

Managing Money Wisely

Do you remember the parable of the talents?[14] Each of the men had something to invest, but they weren't equally efficient in managing what they had. It is good to remember that everything we have comes from God and should be handled with care. This includes our money and possessions, but also our skills, abilities, opportunities, and even our children.

There is a wealth of advice available for people who want to manage their money well: start by tithing 10 percent of your income, save at least something from every paycheck, avoid credit-card buying, try not to borrow. One writer has suggested that it is helpful to:

—Set your financial objectives. What things are most important for you?
—Rank your priorities. What do you want first and what must wait until later?
—Develop a spending plan. Write down your annual income, then make a note of your total giving, your fixed expenses (like mortgage and taxes), and your other expenses. Try to set a realistic budget and stick to it.

—Keep accurate records. This is time-consuming but important. Not only do records help at tax time, but they let you see where your money is going and how accurate your plan has been. If necessary, change the plan. Flexibility is important.[15]

Committing Money Completely

There is no place in the New Testament where we are instructed to give God 10 percent of our income, although this is the usual meaning of the word "tithe." The Hebrews gave much more than that, and in the Old Testament when the people withheld their contributions they were called robbers.[16]

God doesn't want a percentage of our money: He wants all of it. All of our money comes from God, all belongs to Him, and all of it should be spent under His direction. Have you ever asked God to give you wisdom in how your money is spent? If you are committed to Him completely, so should your money be committed. Strange as it may seem, many Christians have discovered that this seeking of divine guidance in money management does much to reduce financial stress.

Work, success, and money—these words symbolize some of the greatest sources of stress in our society. How we cope with these stresses says much about our faith and our values. And how we cope determines to a large extent how we deal in general with the stresses of life.

Chapter 9
LIFE STRESS

In 1941, during the dreadful time of the most intense bombing of London, a British clergyman began the task of translating parts of the New Testament into a language which his war-weary parishioners would understand. "We were," the translator wrote later, "Christians in danger, and since much of the message of the New Testament Epistles is addressed to Christians in danger, I felt that here was an additional reason for putting them into English which could readily be inderstood."[1]

The first book to be completed was Colossians, and when C.S. Lewis, the well-known writer, saw this new version he wrote a letter of congratulations. "It is like seeing an old picture which has been cleaned," Lewis wrote, and he urged that other books of the Bible be put into modern English as quickly as possible.

Thus began the impressive writing career of J.B. Phillips. Unlike so many others, whose writing brings hardly a ripple of appreciation, Phillips discovered that his fresh new wording of the Bible was a dramatic and immediate success. Book sales mushroomed not just in England but around the world, and the name of J.B. Phillips became better and better known. He went on trips that would never have been possible with his parish salary. He received honors and VIP treatment wherever he went, and there were interviews with the press.

Then something happened. It was something, to use Phillips' own words, "which I did not see until it was too late. Satan was mounting his most devastating attack on me. He was building an *image* of 'J.B. Phillips' that was not Jack Phillips at all. I was no longer an ordinary human being; I was in danger of becoming the super-Christian! Everything I wrote or said had to be better than the last. The image grew and grew until it was so unlike me that I could no longer live with it. And yet the thought of destroying it was terrifying too. It was on this dilemma that I hung."[2]

Before long, Dr. Phillips noticed a drying up of his flow of creativity, and he struggled with irrational fears and discouragement. God seemed to be remote, unapproachable, and not available to help.

J.B. Phillips had become a star. Subtly, probably without much awareness, he had begun to build a monument to his own career. Pride and the acclaim of others had taken over as controlling forces in his life. Little wonder that God had become remote and that life had become filled with stress. It was only when Phillips let go of the ego-building drives that his vitality and creativity returned.

Every one of us has similar struggles as we go through life. Unlike Phillips, we may never have to cope with the "subtle and insidious dangers of success," but we all struggle with pride and with the pressures of trying to meet someone else's expectations. Most of us have encountered periods of life when we feel almost overwhelmed—just with the challenge of living and doing our work.

Pressure Points of Life

Over 25 years ago, a psychologist published his list of the stresses that most of us encounter as we go through life. If you look at Table 2 you will notice that with one or two exceptions these events are generally not thought of as crises at all. They are the pressure points of life—problems we must surmount in our earthly pilgrimage if we are to avoid being overwhelmed and emotionally crippled.

YOUTHFUL STRESSES

Literally hundreds of books have been written to analyze each stage of life from conception to death.[3] A small army of psychologists, sociologists, teachers, writers, researchers, and others have tried to find out what is normal development, how people of all ages adapt when things are not normal, and what each of us should do to adapt more effectively.

During the first two decades of life our major task is learning how to fit into a complicated, evolving world. This is a task which at first must be accomplished without the use of language, since babies do not understand the language of their parents, and since it takes several years for children to express themselves fluently and accurately. Even as they move through the teenage years, young people have difficulty finding words to express their inner tensions and needs. The problem is complicated when parents do not encourage such verbal expressions of what is going on inside.

But children need help in coping with the stresses of growing up, and when they can't talk about their needs they show their feelings in other ways. It is easy for parents to understand the distressed cry of a baby with wet diapers, but the "cry" of a schoolboy or teenager is harder to detect and interpret.

In our house, when one of our daughters was about eight, she became "bosom buddies" with another little girl in the neighborhood. Then, without much prior warning, the neighbor girl's father accepted a position in another state and the family prepared to move. In their house and ours we each noticed a little girl struggling with the pain of coming separation. For almost no apparent reason, these little girls, in their own homes, would break out into tears and cry uncontrollably. At first we thought our daughter must be sick or "going through a stage," but then we realized what was happening. Unable to express her stress in words, she was literally crying out for encouragement, reassurance,

——— TABLE 2 ———
POTENTIAL LIFE STRESSES

EARLY CHILDHOOD:
- Learning to experience light and temperature
- Learning to understand others and to communicate needs
- Learning to take solid foods
- Learning to crawl, then walk
- Learning to control the elimination of body wastes
- Learning to talk
- Learning sex differences and modesty
- Learning to understand and face reality
- Learning to relate to parents, siblings, and other people
- Learning to distinguish right from wrong
- Developing a conscience

MIDDLE CHILDHOOD:
- Learning the physical skills needed for ordinary games
- Building a positive self-concept
- Learning to get along with peers
- Learning an appropriate masculine or feminine social role
- Developing skills in reading, writing, speaking, and calculating
- Learning to tell time and to develop skills for everyday living
- Developing conscience, morality, and a scale of values
- Learning a concept of God
- Achieving personal independence
- Developing attitudes toward social groups and institutions

ADOLESCENCE:
- Achieving new and more mature relationships with age mates of both sexes
- Attaining a masculine or feminine social role
- Accepting one's physique and using the body effectively
- Learning to live with and control sexual urges
- Achieving emotional independence of parents and other adults

Selecting and preparing for an occupation

Preparing for marriage and family life

Developing intellectual skills and succeeding in academic pursuits

Desiring and achieving socially responsible behavior

Acquiring a set of values, religious beliefs, and ethics as a guide to behavior

EARLY ADULTHOOD:

Selecting a mate and learning to live with a marriage partner

Adjusting sexually

Starting a family

Rearing children

Acquiring and managing a home

Starting and establishing an occupation

Finding a congenial social group

MIDDLE ADULTHOOD:

Achieving adult civic and social responsibility

Establishing and maintaining an economic standard of living

Raising children and assisting them to become responsible and happy adults

Developing leisure-time activities

Relating to one's spouse as a person

Accepting and adjusting to the physiological changes of middle age

Adjusting to aging parents

Accepting and adjusting to one's degree of vocational success

LATER ADULTHOOD:

Adjusting to declining physical strength and health

Adjusting to death of spouse and peers

Adjusting to retirement and reduced income

Adjusting to the independence of one's children

Adjusting to grandchildren

Meeting social and civic obligations

Establishing satisfactory living arrangements

Preparing for death

and security from her parents at a time when her closest friend was leaving.

Anger, complaining, sulking, criticism of parents, tears, striking out physically, teenage violence, sexual misdemeanors—all of these can be warning signals of turmoil within and of cries for help. The natural response of sensitive parents is to talk and reason together with their children. This can often be helpful, especially if such open communication is something which the children have experienced since their early years. But there are times when the young person is too ashamed, confused, or emotionally upset to talk. These are times for support, encouragement, and the demonstration that parents really care.

This is also a time for strength and control. No matter how long children argue and complain because nobody understands them, they still want someone to be strong and tell them where the lines are drawn. If children or teenagers have no controls they give in too quickly to their impulses and unrestrained curiosity. It scares them when there are no controls or clear standards, but it is reassuring when the adult world says, "You may go so far and no farther. You may have the freedom to do what you want within these limits, but that is as far as you can go."

Under the guidance of sensitive adults, young people learn ways to cope with disappointment, failure, and separation. They master the stresses of adjusting to school, inconsiderate classmates, dating problems, and sexual urges. As they approach adulthood, they struggle with questions like "Who am I?" "What do I believe?" and "What are my standards of right and wrong?"

In many ways, therefore, the first two decades are a training ground—a time of preparation for the stresses which come with adulthood. If a child can learn to cope in childhood and is helped by adults and is not overwhelmed by the stresses of youth, then he or she will cope more effectively after leaving the nest. If childhood has been a series of failures, adulthood often brings more of the same.

GETTING INTO THE ADULT WORLD

One of the most interesting studies of adulthood has been done at Yale University under the direction of psychologist Daniel J. Levinson. According to this research (and our own personal experience) life is not a smooth journey after we leave the tumultuous years of adolescence. Instead, says Dr. Levinson, there are several distinct stages of adulthood, each with its own challenges and each with its unique stresses.

The stages begin in the twenties with a period called "Getting Into the Adult World." This is when a man or woman has pretty much broken away from home and becomes independent in terms of work, friends and perhaps values. But these years involve some very important discussions: if, when, and whom to marry, for example, or the choice of a career. It is a time to take charge of one's life and, free of parental restraints, to start moving toward future goals.

Very often, people in their twenties choose a "mentor," an older friend who can give encouragement, help, friendship, and direction. The foreman who patiently brings a young apprentice to journeyman status or the pastor who helps a young seminary student are examples of mentors. I remember having one of these—a physician who was available when I wanted to talk over lunch but who didn't push himself into my life. He may never have known it, but he helped me find direction in life.

Settling Down

Roughly in the late twenties or early thirties, there is a move into stage two, "settling down." Here, having "found oneself," there is now a willingness to become committed to such life goals as building a career, caring for a family, or accepting responsibilities in the community.

This is not an easy time. Marriage and family life sometimes turn out to be less satisfying than expected. For some people it may be the first real recognition that they will never even get married. At this point comes the first inkling that one's career might be less successful than hoped, and often there is loneliness and fear of failure.

In a recent interview Dr. Levinson was asked how a wife can help her husband through these and future pressures in adult life. "To help her husband," he replied, "she has to be able to join him in his problems. It's not enough for her to find new ways to look nice, or to try to be sexier. She has to recognize the despair he may be feeling and she has to be willing, for example, to let her husband tell her how lousy he thinks their marriage is or how frustrated he feels. This can be very painful for a wife, especially when the husband fails to recognize that wives struggle with marriage and careers too—and women need encouragement, understanding and a listening ear every bit as much as men."4

BOOM-BOOW

The third stage of adulthood usually comes in the late thirties and has been called "Becoming One's Own Man," or BOOM for short. In many respects the abbreviation is accurate because this can be an explosive stage for men, and probably for a woman too, struggling to "Become One's Own Woman."

Very often there is a feeling of being boxed in by the job, by one's marriage, by the family, or by a dead church. The result is an effort to break out and to experience a new sense of freedom. Sometimes at this period women, but especially men, have secret affairs and may leave the family for somebody else. Even those who remain faithful find that their minds begin to wander and that they are more "turned on" by sexual fantasies than they were a few years before.

The same thing occurs at work. There is a special push to attain success, and sometimes this means a mid-life change of career. It is as if the individual somehow realizes that if he or she is to be considered successful by the world and the family it is "now or never."

THE CRISIS OF MIDDLE LIFE

Carl Gustav Jung, the famous Swiss psychiatrist, once described middle age as a time of supreme importance; a period when the second half of our earthly pilgrimage begins. It can be the beginning of great creativity and satisfaction, Jung observed, but middle age can also bring frustration, disappointment, and the realization that we aren't going to succeed as we had hoped.

Very often there is a crisis point, a "midlife crisis," to use the familiar term suggested by Dr. Levinson. Often there is an event in life which, in future years, we look back to as a gentle or abrupt turning point: we are passed over for a promotion, we attain some award, we take up a hobby, or perhaps we simply hear a speech which suddenly causes us to face up to where we are.

The thing that makes midlife a stressful crisis is the awareness of a gap between what we are and what we had hoped to be. Males, for example, women in the labor force, and spouses must come to grips with the fact that they or their mates will never be famous, wealthy, or successful to the degree that they had hoped. We begin to realize that there might be some truth in the words of Sir William Osler, the great physician who once said that "the effective, moving, vitalizing work of the world is done between the ages of 25 and 40." This realization can be demoralizing and discouraging, especially if there are the telltale signs of graying hair, expanding waistlines, decreasing vigor, and children who are leaving the nest.

Writing from the perspective of a middle-aged woman, Eda LeShan described the frustration this way: "While our children have all their choices before them, and can make what they will of their lives, we are facing the unfulfilled dreams of our lives, the mistaken decisions and choices, the things left undone, probably never to be done, we feel. The whole of life is opening to our children just at the same moment when we are having our first terrors that life is closing off for us."[5] It isn't surprising that people in this time of life withdraw into fantasy or lash out with increased work or new romantic ventures which temporarily dull the reality of coming old age.

Even success in life does not protect us from middle-age stress. It's lonely at the top of a business or profession. Sometimes we don't feel appreciated, and there is always the fear that we might make a mistake and fall from our position. Sometimes we get so anxious about this that we aren't careful. We take on too many responsibilities, neglect the family, get careless in our work, and bring on the very things we have been dreading.

Fun at Forty

All of this sounds pretty discouraging, and for many people it is. But in spite of the stress, life doesn't have to end at forty, or at any other age.

A couple of years ago I found myself facing middle age, and on my fortieth birthday I marched into class and told my students to put away their psychology books. "Today," I announced, "I want to tell you what it is like to be forty."

I confessed that I felt some nostalgia, some longing for the agility and irresponsibility of years gone by. But for me the approach of middle life was fun. I have found a loving wife and have a fine family; my work is challenging and growing even though I realize that some of my goals will never be reached; I have friends who respect me and a God who loves me. I am grateful to God, I told my students, for His guidance and goodness in my life.

Perhaps I had reached middle age with a new sense of exhilaration because I met my midlife crisis a year or two early. I had blocked out a big portion of time to write a book, but was delayed for six weeks because my resource materials had been lost in the mail. Far away from home, I literally had nothing to do. Our monthly check had also been delayed, and since we had no money to spend we could only pass the time walking and thinking.

During those weeks I reevaluated my whole life, setting some of my goals lower and pondering my future. What did I want to accomplish? How would I get there? What were the ultimate goals for our family?

This kind of reevaluation has to come at some time during the middle years. Suppose you've gone about as far as you can go in your job. Think, then, how life can be rewarding during the years ahead. Develop your interests (along new lines, if you wish), face up to your limitations, and set some realistic goals for your future. Determine to work on your marriage to make it more enriching.

Remember too that God has a plan for every life, and that this plan doesn't just cover the first four decades of your existence. Some of the greatest men in the Bible (Noah, for example, and Moses) did the most for God in their later years, after they had passed forty. Middle age today can be a time of stress and reevaluation, or it can be the beginning of a new, more relaxed period of life.

Restabilization

This brings us to what Levinson's Yale research group calls the stage of "Restabilization and the End of the Mid-Life Decade." Most of us make some changes in our life-style—if only to slow down—but we are also likely to keep the same marriage, the same job, and the same way of life. We put our emphases on those parts of our lives which are fulfilling and we reconcile ourselves to that which will never be attained. As we enter the fifties we more or less settle down until we come to the next major stress point: retirement and old age.

BECOMING A SENIOR CITIZEN

Old age doesn't have a very good image in our society. We assume, for example, that old people have brains through which recent names, dates, and memories regularly slip away. We decide that since we can't "teach old dogs new tricks," old people can't learn very well. We conclude that the aged lack creativity, dwell on the past, are slow and plodding, tend to be ultraconservative, have no interest in sex, constantly complain, and are dependent on others for all kinds of help.

This is a grim picture, and most of it isn't true. Nevertheless, we dread the later years because this is the period of life when we are old in a culture which idolizes youth, when we are in failing health among a people who value physical fitness, when we are unable to work in a society which measures worth in terms of productivity, and when we are a reminder of coming death in a culture where death is something we try to hide.

During the first fifteen years of my life I had an aged grandfather who lived in our home. He never said much about old age, but even as a boy I learned about his difficulties, and long after his death I found myself writing a master's thesis and doctoral dissertation on the stresses of aging.

The list of these stresses is long: loneliness, feelings of uselessness, loss of a mate, sadness over the deaths of longtime friends, declining health, boredom, and financial struggles, to name a few. Some of these events leave us changed permanently, but even then there are ways to meet the stresses of later life. We can prepare, accept, and reevaluate.

Prepare

It seems simple, and it's extremely important, but hardly anyone deliberately gets ready for old age. Perhaps it's a part of an ostrich mentality which keeps our heads buried in the sand in hopes that old age won't creep up on us if we don't see it. When Paul Tournier, in his mid-seventies, was asked to write a book on aging, he suggested that we must prepare for retirement well in advance—in our fifties or, even better, in our forties.[6]

The way to prepare, Tournier suggested, is to develop a second career. This involves developing interests and skills during the working years which can expand to provide interesting and useful activities after our first career is over. The older we get, the harder it is to find new interests, so we should start early.

Many businesses and communities, along with a few alert churches, are providing pre-retirement instruction for older workers. This helps them to anticipate future problems and to discuss ways in which the problems of older persons can be faced. The stresses of aging, like all other stresses, are less devastating and easier to tackle when they are anticipated.

Have you ever wondered what you will be like in old age? Will you be bitter, cynical, and angry with the world, or will you have a happy disposition with a positive outlook on life? You will get along much better if you are cheerful than if you are grumpy. For one thing, people will enjoy your presence and you will be less lonely. Remember, however, that you don't get a new disposition with retirement. Cheerful old people were once cheerful young people, and complaining, miserable old people griped when they were young too. Perhaps one of the best ways to prepare for the stresses of age is to start looking at the positive things in life[7] and asking God to mold us into warm, loving, people-centered individuals—now.

Accept

It's a common human tendency, I suppose, but we often avoid facing unpleasant or threatening situations for as long as we can. Going on a diet, having the long-awaited surgery, facing the fact that our marriage is in trouble, writing the sensitive letter—all of these and hundreds of others are examples of procrastination in the face of difficulties.

Nowhere is this more prevalent than in old age. We try to ignore the changes in our bodies and we assume, almost unconsciously, that we are somewhat invulnerable. We know that others around us grow old and that we will too, but somehow we like to think that our same age peers look and act a lot older than we do, or that we (unlike them) will still make it to that great unfulfilled goal that we may have in life.

We will get along better if we openly acknowledge those things that we cannot change and change those things that we can. This is the real meaning of acceptance. How do you react when retirement ends your career, or poor health ends your tennis game, or your married child moves away? You can mope and feel sorry for yourself, or you can go on to get involved with people and make the best of a difficult situation.

Twenty years ago, back in the days when rich people flew across the Atlantic and poor people took the boat, I was on a ship where I met a retired English couple returning home after a visit to North America. We soon became friends and began a correspondence which continues to this day. Although the man has been dead for many years, I continue to correspond with his widow and still see her occasionally. Happily, this lady, now in her late eighties, is able to get around. How does she spend her time? She works for a volunteer agency preparing and delivering hot meals for old people. She reminds me of a former teaching colleague of mine whose specialty was mathematics. He is spending his later years helping other retired persons complete their income tax returns. These are people who have adapted to the stresses of age by openly acknowledging their declining status in life and by doing whatever they can with the strength and abilities that remain.

Reevaluate

Dr. James E. Birren, director of the Ethel Andrus Gerontology at the University of Southern California, has suggested that older persons need to constantly reevaluate where they are in life.[8] It's easy to put off this evaluation, waiting for a more convenient time, but, says Dr. Birren, "for everyone there finally comes that point when you realize you've hit your plateau. You are where you are, and you have to accept life as you've lived it." Regretfully, that realization makes some people bitter, and then they become sour, depressed, and withdrawn. It is far better to create new goals and to take another look at the meaning of life.

James Birren had another suggestion: "The key to the aging process is learning the art of communication." That means learning to listen and taking an interest in people, who is turn will be interested in you.

THE MEANING OF LIFE

Shakespeare once described life as "a tale told by an idiot, full of sound and fury, signifying nothing." For many people this may be an accurate description. Certainly we encounter a variety of stresses as we go through life, and, even though these challenge us, they are also frustrating.

The Bible has some things to say about life and its stresses. Life is described as being like a vapor that appears for a while and then vanishes away.[9] Life is something temporary, but it can also be fulfilling, and for the believer in Jesus Christ life is only a prelude to *eternal* life following our earthly death.[10]

The Apostle Paul was a man who had experienced life in its fullest. He had been born into a wealthy religious family with good parents and a superb education. He became a religious leader and enjoyed considerable prestige in the synagogues until he became a Christian on the road to Damascus. Then Paul's troubles really began—criticism, beatings, rejection, shipwreck, imprisonment.

In one of his last letters, however, he shows that in spite of the stresses, life had been worth it all. "Christ shall even now, as always, be exalted in my body, whether by life or by death," he wrote from prison.[11] If I live, that will be great, he said in essence, but if I die, that's okay too, because I will be with Christ.

This is the real answer to life stresses—asking the God of the universe to guide our steps, actions, decisions, and attitudes at every stage in life. When we commit life to God and acknowledge His leadership in every area of life, He *will* direct our steps.[12] This doesn't mean that stress will be eliminated, for to eliminate stress is to remove life. But it does means that life pressures are more tolerable. Like Paul, we can live enveloped by joy despite life's stresses.

Chapter 10
CRISIS STRESS

Late one night during the spring of 1943, the sirens of London sounded to warn of still another enemy attack on the British capital. As had been their custom for so many months, the weary Londoners hurried to the relative safety of those many air raid shelters which had protected them from destruction since the start of World War Two.

In one part of the city, six hundred people crowded together in a shelter near their homes and settled down to wait out the attack. Suddenly their underground haven was abruptly jolted as a bomb exploded nearby. Immediately the lights went out and everything went silent. There was no yelling and no crying, and as the rescue workers discovered when they reached the scene later, there were no injuries. But two hundred people were dead. Autopsies showed that although these people had not been hurt, they had been so overcome by fear that they had stopped breathing. These people had literally been scared to death.

The bombing of one's city is a crisis, and so is death in the family, divorce, serious sickness, or the unexpected loss of a job. These don't come along very often, and some of us avoid most of these stresses altogether. When they do come, however, they hit with special force. Because they are so novel, we aren't really sure how to react, but the stress is so overwhelming that we have to do something and do it soon. In this chapter we will discuss some of the major stress-producing crises of life: losing a job, getting a divorce, being in an accident, getting sick, and facing death.

UNEMPLOYMENT: THE LOSS OF WORK

What does the term "unemployed" suggest to you? Perhaps you think of people too lazy to work or men and women who have so little education and so few skills that they can't find employment. Such people, however, comprise only a small part of those without jobs. In addition there are:

—students and housewives who need money to make ends meet but cannot find work;

—carpenters, farm workers, and other skilled laborers whose jobs are tied to the weather and who are idle during certain periods of the year;

—highly educated teachers and scientists who are trained for fields of work that are already overstocked with people;

—disabled persons who want work but are physically unable;

—business executives who at the age of forty or fifty are suddenly let go from a job and are unable to find another;

—willing workers who get laid off because the economy is bad, or because there is no demand for the employer's product, or because a strike somewhere has forced a slowdown in production.

All of these people, and others like them, are unemployed and looking for work.

The Stresses of Unemployment

It's a stressful thing to be out of work, especially if you have been fired. There is a feeling of discouragement and anger, followed by a great loss of self-esteem. Unemployment means that you have failed to meet the expectations of yourself, your family, and perhaps your boss. In a society which values productivity and measures people's worth by their success, it is easy to feel that you are unimportant. Little wonder that jobless people often experience pity and a sense of futility. It's even worse if you have previously had an important position.

Consider, for example, the highly paid executive who loses his job. If he is over forty, unemployed, and accustomed to a high salary, it is almost impossible for him to find another position that compares with the one he left. When he goes for unemployment compensation he experiences humiliation and bureaucratic red tape. This may be made worse by the "mightier than thou" attitude of the civil servants at the unemployment office, who are accustomed to dealing with chronically unemployed and psychologically helpless people. It isn't surprising that, while unemployment stresses can be intense for everyone, they are especially difficult for the person who has come from a high-status, previously secure position.[1]

In our culture, unemployed people are surplus people who often feel unwanted by society. When you are out of work, your lifestyle, goals, expectations, social life, financial status, appearance, and self-image all change. Research reports show that most people develop a cynicism toward society which persists even after they find another job and return to work.[2] In the absence of significant research, one can only wonder how unemployment of the breadwinner affects the spouse and family.

Meeting the Jobless Stresses

Somehow we must demolish the idea that our worth as individuals depends on our status and success as workers. God doesn't evaluate people that way and neither must we.

It is true that many unemployed people *are* educationally and psychologically incapable of holding a job, but large numbers of jobless people do not fit this category. Those of us who are employed must treat the unemployed with respect and friendship. Continue to welcome them into your circles and try to avoid asking, "Did you get a job yet?" A question like "How are things going?" is more tactful, expresses both interest and concern, and also saves face for the person who is still jobless.

The family of the unemployed person is an important key to the whole crisis of unemployment. Unemployment leads to increased tension in the home (all of the family is affected), but if the family members can be understanding and mutually helpful, these difficult times can be handled effectively and may even be enriching.

Finding Work

A loss of work presents us with the challenge of undertaking a thorough self-evaluation. Alone or with your spouse ask such questions as "What do I want to do?" "What am I trained to do?" "What do I do best?" "What is the existing job market?" and "How should I go about finding work?"

Then do some research—in the classified ads of the newspaper, in the local employment office, in the union files, in the college placement office, and in the trade journals (available at your local library). Watch for newspaper or magazine articles which might be helpful in job-hunting. Your local library might help here too.

For the better-paying jobs it helps to prepare a resume—a short, concise, accurate summary of your education, experience, and special skills. Be honest without demeaning yourself or overselling yourself. Send the resume with a covering letter to the personnel office of different companies and follow up with a phone call requesting an interview. Realize that you will be turned down frequently or ignored, but keep looking. In addition, don't overlook your friends who might hear of unadvertised jobs, and in all of this be honest and be yourself. Nothing is more easily spotted than a phony, especially in a job interview.

In all of this we must remember the awesome power of prayer. God meets our needs, He leads us in our paths, and He is able to lead us back to employment.

DIVORCE: THE LOSS OF A MATE

"Soaring Divorce Rates: Our National Disgrace." "The American Way of Marriage—Divorce and Remarriage." "Divorce Rate Increases."

These headlines are common these days, and their message is even more familiar: increasing numbers of marriages are breaking up. The divorce statistics differ, depending on where you live, but the instability of marriage appears to be part of our modern way of life.

What happens when a marriage begins to crumble and fall apart? Invariably there is stress, especially on the part of the husband, wife, and children, but also on the couple's relatives and friends. Marriage breakups proclaim that a couple has failed in interpersonal relationships. They are unwilling or unable to get along. Rejection, loneliness, discouragement, difficulties in trying to make it alone, self-pity, insecurity, financial problems, sexual frustrations—all of these and more are likely to appear when separation occurs. Then there are the feelings of anger, bitterness, and jealousy, all of which can lead to guilt.

In reality, divorce is a grief reaction. Even though you may have agreed to the decision to separate, there is still a sense of loss and a slow emotional adjustment to the idea that "it's all over" and you are single again. Unlike the pain of death, when you see the coffin and grave at the funeral, the divorced mate is still around, perhaps enjoying life—a constant reminder of your marriage failure.

Divorce is a great stress on children as well as on their parents, and according to one report the children often react with *anger* directed toward one or both of the parents, *guilt* over the part they might have played in the divorce, feelings of *rejection*, and sometimes *fear* of being left alone or forsaken.[3] Such children need special attention, and will often act out their insecurities with misbehavior. The misbehavior becomes an unconscious testing to see if there really are limits and some lines of stability.

Friends don't always help either. While some are kind

and supportive, others are overly gushy in their attempts to be useful, many are critical, and a few just disappear. The church, rather than offering support and love, too frequently shows criticism and rejection. For some of these well-meaning but insensitive people, divorce is the unpardonable sin.

Who Am I?

Perhaps one of the greatest stresses following divorce is the loss of self-esteem and a struggle to discover "Who am I?" Consider the woman first. She is no longer somebody's wife. She may not be sure how she will be received in society as a divorcee, and for many women there is the struggle of reentering the labor force, perhaps for the first time in years, or learning to raise the children alone.

If he gets the children, it is the husband who faces the stress of a single-parent family. He must adapt to the role of ex-husband with an ex-wife, and often he discovers that the life of a "carefree bachelor" isn't as carefree as many people suspect.

An Ounce of Prevention

The best way to prevent the strain of divorce is, of course, to build a marriage which is growing instead of dying. This isn't always easy, however, and we all know of situations where a spouse walks in one day and announces that the marriage is over. At this point it doesn't help at all to tell such people what they should have done to make their marriage work.

Separated and divorced people need someone to talk to and a shoulder to cry on. They need to be loved, accepted, forgiven, and welcomed in the church. Some could use help in such practical issues as balancing the budget, adjusting to a new lifestyle, finding a job, or handling the children alone.

The divorced person also needs to spend time analyzing. Why did my marriage fail? What could I have done differently? How can I improve in the future? Where do I go from here?

In his book *Creative Divorce*,[4] Mel Krantzler suggests that the divorced person should work to avoid the following emotional traps, each of which can prolong the stress. These are traps, incidentally, which can prolong stress in a number of areas, not just divorce.

Self-fulfilling prophecies. Here you make a decision about what will happen (e.g., "I'll never be happy again"), and then you unconsciously arrange to make your prediction come true.

Unwarranted generalizations. If you keep repeating statements like "no man can be trusted" or "all women are possessive," you will eventually come to believe what you tell yourself, thereby preventing yourself from being proven wrong.

Unrealistic expectations. When you set your goals so high that failure is inevitable (e.g., "If I can't find a perfect mate, I'll have no part of marriage"), you are bound to be miserable.

Disastering. This involves looking for and expecting the worst. Along comes one piece of bad news and you have "proof" that things will always be bad.

Wallowing. This follows easily from disastering and involves feeling sorry for oneself, refusing to try anything risky, and apparently enjoying the misery.

Blame-making. Instead of facing one's own problems and failures there is a tendency to push the blame onto someone else. Ask instead, "What did I do wrong that I need not do again?"

Running. This assumes that since the cause of problems exists apart from ourselves, the solution must be external too. As a result we change jobs, move, or start somewhere else, all the while failing to recognize that we cannot run away from problems, since most of our problems arise from within.

Living through others. This is a common reaction of people who are alone. They cling tenaciously to other people and find in others (their children, for example) their only reason for living. This is almost certain to lead to disappointment and rejection by the people (including the children) who feel the clenches of a lonely other person.

Yearnings of a half person. Here is the idea that life can be fulfilled only if there is another person "to make me whole again." Such thinking prevents the divorced person from developing his or her own strengths as an independent adult.

Jesus and Divorce

When Jesus was confronted by a group of religious leaders one day, He took a pretty hard line on divorce.[5] It isn't within God's plan for married people to separate, He said, and only when adultery is involved can we reluctantly agree that divorce is permitted.

On another occasion, however, Jesus met a woman who had had five husbands and even then was living with a man to whom she was not married.[6] The Bible doesn't say she was divorced, but that might be a logical assumption. At no time did Jesus say that the woman's behavior was all right—that would have been inconsistent with His teaching elsewhere—but He did show compassion. He met her need, and before long she was an active Christian.

It may sound trite, but it is a profoundly moving truth that Jesus Christ meets the needs of divorced people today. He has told us to cast our burdens on Him[7], and He also meets our needs by providing guidance, peace, and wisdom in the times of stress. Perhaps this is especially true in situations like divorce, where all too often there are few others around to help.

SICKNESS: THE LOSS OF HEALTH

A few months ago our neighbor died. Everybody

pretended it wasn't happening, but as the cancer enveloped her body she became weaker and weaker until there was no strength left.

I wonder if her early death could have been prevented. Several years earlier she had noticed a lump on her breast, but she tried to forget it. Her mother had died of cancer at an early age, but my neighbor was afraid to visit a doctor lest she hear the dreaded diagnosis. Apparently she waited too long.

Anxiety over Sickness

Almost everyone has heard of hypochondriacs. These are people who have an excessive concern over their health, who worry over the most minor physical problems, and who seem unable to accept the reassurance from others that everything is okay. More than anything else, these people are anxious and could profit from some long talks with a friend or counselor about the reasons for their anxieties.

Most of us do not fit the hypochondriac category, but we do feel apprehensive about physical disease, especially if we have symptoms which we can't explain. "What if I'm *really* sick?" we might think to ourselves, or "What if I had to go into the hospital?"

Illness can be a stressful experience. Even the "24-hour flu" can disrupt routines, create anxiety, and leave us physically weak. But what if the sickness is more severe—cancer, for example, or heart disease? What if there are undiagnosed symptoms which persist in spite of medication? These are especially stressful because we don't know what is happening to our bodies, and because the likelihood of complete recovery is uncertain. It is then that we begin to worry about pain, uncomfortable treatment, techniques, temporary or permanent incapacity, financial strain, or the influence of our illness on the family.

Surgery

If the sick person is hospitalized, the stress is even greater. Pulled from loved ones and familiar surroundings when you need them most, you become "a patient." You are now an impersonal resident in a hospital bed, cared for by people who might be warm and cheerful but who are nevertheless strangers doing things to your body that usually you do for yourself.

Irving Janis, whose studies of surgical patients were mentioned in Chapter 4, has suggested that

> From a psychological standpoint, a major surgical operation constitutes a stress situation which resembles many other types of catastrophies and disasters in that the "victim" faces a combination of three major forms of imminent danger—the possibility of suffering acute pain, of undergoing serious body damage, and of dying.[8]

There are great individual differences in the way we handle the stress of surgery or other physical illness. According to Dr. Janis, we handle sickness best when we have had an "emotional inoculation" beforehand.

Emotional Inoculation

An inoculation, of course, involves the injection of a mild virus into the body. As it fights off this mild virus, the body is mobilized to cope with a more serious disease which might appear later. As we indicated in Chapter 4, the same thing can happen psychologically. If, prior to surgery or other medical treatment, a normal person is given accurate information about the coming pain, discomfort, or inconveniences, then the stress is more bearable when it comes. Research studies have shown,[9] however, that these prior warnings must come with reassurances, so that the person is not thrown into panic. It also helps if the person under stress can have information which he or she can use for self-reassurance.

Several years ago an interesting experiment was conducted at the Massachusetts General Hospital.[10] Roughly one hundred surgical patients were divided into two groups which were similar in terms of age, sex, type of operation, etc. Each of the patients was visited before surgery by an anesthetist who gave routine information about the operation—its time, the nature of anesthesia, etc. In addition, the patients in one group—let's call them the emotionally inoculated group—were told what to expect in the way of pain after the operation, were given reassurance that such pain is normal, were advised how to relax abdominal muscles so the pain would be less severe, and were assured that they would be given medication if the pain became intolerable. In order to make sure that all one hundred patients got the same medical treatment, neither the nurses nor the doctors were told about the experiment.

What happened? When compared to the other group, the emotionally inoculated patients required far less pain medication after surgery, were more cheerful and cooperative with the hospital staff, complained less, and were released from the hospital several days sooner than the other group.

Is it possible, some have asked, to inoculate people emotionally so they are better prepared to face the stresses of divorce, death of a loved one, the start of a new job, career failure, or other crises? Apparently the answer is yes. The United States Peace Corps, for example, provides emotional inoculation for people going overseas, and progressive missionary societies do the same. It's difficult, but to some extent an individual can do some self-inoculation—getting information before a coming crisis situation, knowing what to expect, and reassuring oneself.

Accidents and Other Unexpected Illness

Sickness, like death, doesn't always come when we expect it, and thus there is often no time for preparation. The accident victim, for example, has to cope not only with pain but with the shock of being immobilized so unexpectedly. Even when we are expecting problems, like surgery, a progressive disease, or a long period of recuperation, it is easy to deny the seriousness of the situation and to hide behind overoptimistic statements which keep us from being afraid. Without this prior preparation, the stresses hit with greater force and the crisis is accompanied by anger and intense fear.

The situation is not hopeless, however. Even when there has been denial and no prior emotional inoculation, the Christian realizes that he or she has a source of hope in Jesus Christ. He has promised to never leave us,[11] and the Bible reassures us that the God of all comfort will bring a deep inner peace into the lives of those who put their confidence in Him.[12] God doesn't always heal, nor does He necessarily take away the pain (although He sometimes does both). Always, however, God makes the pain bearable and gives the inner assurance that He is with us, helping with the stresses of life. This inner strength is even more apparent when we face the stresses of death.

DEATH: THE LOSS OF LIFE

Bob is a friend of mine who is dying. He knows it, his wife knows it, and his friends know it. He was in his midtwenties, still a student, when he first noticed the symptoms. Learning that he had cancer was hard to take, but after the shock, Bob and his wife decided to live life to its fullest and to make the best of the time that remained. Bob's strength is waning, and there has to be time for chemotherapy and other treatment, but he is still alive, pastoring a little church in the West and ministering to the needs of others. He's also open about his condition and bleak chance for survival.

"Every day when I get up," he stated recently, "I thank God for sparing me through another night, and I live with the full realization that this day may be my last."

Denying Death

It's refreshing to find somebody that honest about death. We live in a death-denying society. Man is the only creature who knows that death is inevitable, but he tries to forget this and, as a result, has trouble handling death when it comes. We don't talk about death, we fail to plan for it, we do everything possible to delay it, and we prefer to forget it. Death, which used to occur in the home surrounded by caring relatives, now takes place in sterile hospitals, where even medical people try to avoid the dying patient as much as possible. "I wanted to talk about my condition," a dying man once told a friend, "but it's hard to carry on a conversation when the doctor puts a stethoscope in his ears and a thermometer in my mouth."

Even when death occurs we do what we can to hide it. We try to soften the horror of death, writes Bayly, "by honoring the corpse. We patch it up, preserve it, dress it in going away clothes, place it on a restful couch, surround it with flowers, arrange the pink, pale lights, burn it or bury it."[13] We talk in soft tones to the survivors but expect them to snap out of their grief quickly and carry on as if nothing had happened.

There may be a variety of reasons for this widespread attempt to forget about death, but surely one factor is the realization that when we think about death we are confronted with one of life's biggest stresses—the fact that we will die someday too. That is very threatening. Death is an enemy which eventually will take us all, but most people prefer to deal with the enemy by not thinking about it.

Helping Others Die

When psychiatrist Elisabeth Kübler-Ross published her bestselling book *On Death and Dying*,[14] she startled a lot of people who had never thought much about dying. "The fear of death is a universal fear," she wrote following her interviews with hundreds of terminally ill patients. Doctors don't like to mention it, family members pretend to hide it, but most (if not all) terminal patients know they are dying, and it would be better for everyone if they courageously discussed it.

In her book, Dr. Kübler-Ross first outlined the five stages of dying which have been found to characterize terminally ill patients who survive for a while following the initial diagnosis. First there is shock and denial ("Oh, no; it can't be me"), and then comes anger, which sometimes lashes out even against the people we love. Bargaining is the third stage, in which the patient tries to make a deal with God ("If I get more time, I'll serve God for the rest of life"). When such denials are no longer convincing there often is depression (stage four) followed by the fifth stage, a quiet acceptance of the inevitable. There are some patients who fight to the end, struggling to avoid death, but for them it is harder to reach the stage of acceptance with peace and dignity. Even so, in every stage there is always hope that a new remedy will be found or that in some other way death will be delayed.

How can we help a person face the stress of dying? We can talk about it, express our fears and frustrations, cry together, and ponder the love of God which has conquered death. Often a dying patient wants to talk about his or her feelings but finds that there are few people who want to talk about death. In one study if was found that the cleaning women, more than anyone else, talked with dying patients about their feelings. Relatives found it too stressful and medical personnel found such talk difficult because of their own feelings of helplessness and failure in the face of terminal illness. Communication, however, is only difficult the first time and becomes easier thereafter. Such open talk helps everyone cope more effectively with the stress of terminal illness.

This is even possible with a child. "Our little boy died at home," writes Joe Bayly.

> He began to bleed at six o'clock in the morning. The doctor came later and said, 'I could put him in the hospital

and he could have a massive transfusion. Maybe he'd live a few days longer, maybe not.'

We chose to have him stay at home, in the familiar bedroom, with his father and mother to comfort him and love him and talk to him about Jesus' love and heaven.

In the previous months, when we knew that he had leukemia—and even before—we had talked naturally about these things and he had responded with the simple faith of a child in what his parents tell him.

Now he didn't want to go to heaven. He wanted to stay with us in the familiar home. (What little boy wants to leave his mother and daddy, his brothers and sister?)

At two-thirty in the afternoon, he died.

Died?

In Jesus' words, 'the angels carried him' to heaven.[15]

Preparing for Death Ourselves

Death is the one inevitable event that we all must face, but most of us never prepare for it. We don't prepare wills, do not have adequate insurance, never discuss our funerals, sometimes give no thought to meeting God after death, and, as we have seen, avoid discussing the reality of our condition when we are ill.

Several months ago, following a visit to the Far East, I left my family in Manila, where they were to get a flight back to North America across the Pacific while I went on to India and home by way of Europe. On the night before our separation my wife and I sat down to discuss what would happen if either of us didn't make it home. This was a hard discussion—stressful, to say the least—but it wasn't morbid. We wanted to help each other to know how to get along without a partner. We didn't want to deny the reality of death, like so many people do, and then leave a grief-stricken family to make important decisions alone. By denying death, refusing to talk about it, avoiding funeral homes even when our friends die, and never thinking about our own death, we are increasing the potential for stress when we come to the end of our own lives and making it more difficult for those who survive after we are gone.

The Stress of Grief

Grief is an emotion, a deep sense of loss which comes whenever we are cut off from contact with someone we have loved. In one sense divorce, homesickness, and the pain of prolonged separation are all grief reactions, but nothing is as final as death itself.[16]

There is no such thing as a normal or typical grief reaction. Each of us experiences grief in a somewhat unique way, but there are some reactions which are extremely common. First, for example, there is shock, a stunned disbelief that comes even when the death was expected. Usually this is a short stage, lasting only a few hours or days.

At some time we begin to be overwhelmed with emotions—sorrow, depression, loneliness, intense longing for the lost person. At first there is value in expressing these emotions, but such catharsis expressions are only part of the process. We need to begin what has been called the "work of mourning": thinking about our past days with the deceased, pondering past joys and sorrows, deciding what we will do next, facing the guilt that we feel, acknowledging the hostility and resentment that we may feel toward the doctors, toward the departed person, and even toward God.

The funeral can help, especially if the mourners are not afraid to cry and can express their love and support for the survivors. Funerals have been criticized in our society for their contribution to the denial of death, but sometimes the presence of the body brings home the reality of the situation and reaffirms the survivors' faith in God and the hereafter.

The work of mourning goes on for many months, however. Every memory of the loved person is likely to be brought up and relived in the mourner's imagination before the work of mourning is complete. Slowly the mourner picks up life again and goes on as best as possible in view of the loved one's departure.

Helping the Grieving

Grief should not be carried on alone. We have a loving God who comforts us directly, but often I think He comforts us through the continuing support, encouragement, and "listening ear" of other people.

At times, mourners like to be left alone, but they also need people—people who love them, help them with the practical realities of living without the deceased, pray with and for them, and remember them in a special way on birthdays, anniversaries, holidays, and other difficult times.

Not long ago I had an older lady in one of my classes who had been a widow for several years. Unknown to me, the day before a big exam this lady reached the thirtieth anniversary of her marriage. "We always went out to dinner on our anniversary," she told one of her classmates, "and it's very lonely to be alone on this day." Several of the class members decided to put aside their books and take the lady out to dinner. She wasn't asking for this and hadn't expected it, but it helped her to see the concern of fellow students who took the time to be present at a time when her grief was especially apparent.

Life After Death

The preceding pages have dealt almost exclusively with the stresses of life, but it would be grossly cruel to the reader if nothing was said about the stresses *after* life is over. We all have an appointment with death, the Bible states, and after this there will be judgment.[17]

Such a conclusion isn't popular today, so millions of people "take their chances" and hope that, if there is a God and a heaven, they can somehow persuade the Almighty to be lenient. That same almighty God has already told us, however, that persuasion at the gates of heaven won't work. We are saved through faith in Jesus Christ. Salvation and an eternal, stress-free life in paradise come as a "gift of God, not as a result of works."[18] The gift is given now and can be received for the taking, but after death it will be too late.

We take the gift of eternal life by confessing our sins in prayer and believing that Jesus Christ is our Savior (from eternal punishment) and Lord.[19]

When Jesus was on earth He often told stories that would make a difficult point clearer. One of these "parables" concerned a self-centered rich man and a devout but poor man named Lazarus. After death, Lazarus went to heaven but the rich man found himself being tormented in hell. "I am in agony," he cried out under the greatest stress possible.

When the rich man learned that there was an uncrossable chasm between heaven and hell, he begged that his brothers would be warned so they wouldn't experience the stress of hell after death. "They've got the Bible," the rich man was told, but he protested that they wouldn't pay attention to the Bible.

The same is true today. There are people (perhaps you) who are struggling to overcome the stresses in life, but oblivious to and unwilling to even accept the possibility of greater stresses after death—stresses which could be avoided altogether by a commitment of our lives to Christ right now in this life. How do *you* plan to respond?

Chapter 11
RELIGIOUS STRESS

Several years ago a disgruntled student came to see me about some problems which seemed to center around one major theme—his dislike of the church. Many church members, he had concluded, were gossips and cynics. He was bothered by phoniness in the church, and by the fact that much of what passed for worship was really meaningless, boring, and routine. Most of all, he complained about the failure of many church people to turn their theology into practice. "They know what they believe," my friend complained, "and they can even quote the Bible, but it doesn't make any difference in their lives. They still fight with their mates, argue with their neighbors, give in to their impulses, and probably cheat on their income tax."

As I talked further with this student I began to see that there were other and more basic problems in his life, but the church came up again and again, and to some extent I had to recognize that his criticisms were valid. In an earlier chapter we quoted the opinion of two writers who stated that "religion in a devout believer has little equal as an allayer of stress." We have returned to this conclusion several times and will do so again. But the fact remains that for many people, religion is a *source* of stress rather than a solution to the problem.

STRESSES FROM RELIGION

Let's go back to this angry young man who so vehemently criticized religion. I suspected (and later confirmed) that he was not as antireligion as he pretended. Sometimes too much protesting about something is an indicator that the protestor is unconsciously attracted to the very thing he or she is condemning. Underneath all the criticism my counselee really saw value in the church, and after expressing his anger he began to reevaluate some of his frustrations.

The Demands of Religion

For many people religion is too stressful because of its demands. During the past century we who are Christians have dealt with this by conveniently overlooking the costs of following Christ. Bonhoeffer wrote about this from his prison cell when he condemned our tendency to believe in what he called "cheap grace." It cost God the excruciating death of His Son to make eternal life possible for us, and although salvation is absolutely free for the asking, with no strings attached, we soon discover that following Jesus can create stresses. For one thing, there is criticism and not-so-subtle rejection. In our society we tolerate almost anything, including Satan worship and occultism, more than we tolerate a dedicated Christian.

In one way this is not surprising, since Jesus never promised that his followers would have an easy life. "It will be tough," He told His disciples; "you will be like sheep among wolves—persecuted, ridiculed, deprived of life's comforts. You will have to take up a cross, the symbol of shame and low status, if you are to follow me." For centuries devout Christians have been persecuted, it's happening today, and the Bible predicts that it will get worse.

If persecution and stress go along with Christianity, why would anybody want to follow Jesus? The answer is that *the difficulties of the Christian walk are far outweighed by the benefits.* Committed Christians know a constant inner peace, a security, and a sense of joy which persists in the midst of life's most intense stress. The Christian also has cause to hope for the future. "In the world you have tribulation," Jesus told His followers, "but take courage; I have overcome the world. . . . Peace I leave with you; My peace I give to you; not as the world gives do I give you. Let not your heart be troubled, nor let it be fearful."[1] The God of the universe has promised to stick with His followers "through thick and thin." That's not a denial of reality; it is a source of intense encouragement in times of stress.

There are many people who call themselves Christian but who have never received the message that while Christ brings an inner comfort, following Jesus is also costly. Such people may be very sincere and even regular churchgoers, but for them God is on the fringes of life. They rarely think about Him, talk about Him even less, almost never pray, and have missed the real inner peace that comes through daily meditation on the Word of God. These people turn to God in crises but largely ignore Him when things are running smoothly. To be honest, all of us have strong tendencies in this direction and find ourselves drifting away from God. When we do so, a host of unnecessary stresses arise, the kinds of stresses in the church which so infuriated my student counselee and so delight those who like to criticize religion.

The Threat to Independence

"Do your own thing" is a popular phrase which is only a few years old, but it reflects a philosophy that has been with us for many years, especially in America. It is the belief in rugged individualism, a conviction that "there's no help needed—I can handle this job all by myself."

Religion is a threat to this way of thinking because it proclaims that men and women are in need of a Savior. We can't really make it on our own, the Bible says—we need help—and to the modern mind this translates to "you are incapable, inferior, and lacking independence."

But the Bible is realistic. It portrays mankind as being created by God in His image, but not powerful enough to bring about our own salvation or to eliminate the stresses of life by ourselves. Commitment to a powerful God frees us to boldly take hold of life and push ahead, secure in the realization that Christ gives us the strength and direction we need. The Christian is not independent; he or she doesn't want to be, for that creates greater stresses and worry about the future. The Christian, however, is free—free to become the person that he or she is capable of becoming, and free of the anxiety which comes when we have no understanding of death, no real belief in the value of life, and no clue about what might happen after we die.

The Problem of Intellectual Respectability

Near the beginning of this century, psychoanalyst Sigmund Freud wrote the first of several stinging attacks on religion, and this antireligious theme has characterized much of psychology ever since. A more contemporary psychologist, for example, has labeled religious people emotionally disturbed, and has argued that religion consists only of "some kind of faith unfounded on fact."[2]

Nobody wants to commit his life and future to some system which is "unfounded on fact." That would give only the most shaky foundation to our existence. It would provide little hope for the future and almost no encouragement in times of pressure. Instead, a faith unfounded on fact would doubtless create more stresses than it would alleviate.

The issue here, however, is what do we mean by "facts"? Facts are past and present events which have been observed by large numbers of people who are in a position to observe them. If we take such a definition, then a system like Christianity is not something "unfounded on fact."

In a thought-provoking and superbly written little book, Dr. Clark H. Pinnock has written this about the Bible and the Christ of Christianity:

There exists no document from the ancient world witnessed by so excellent a set of textual and historical testimonies, and offering so superb an array of historical data on which an intelligent decision may be made. An honest man cannot dismiss a source of this kind. Skepticism regarding the historical credentials of Christianity is based upon an irrational bias.

Christianity is Christ. It is only appropriate to begin with Him when investigating the claims of the Christian gospel. He is the center both of our theology and apologetics. In addition, He is almost universally admired and respected for His wisdom, His character, and His beneficial effect upon the world. An intelligent non-Christian owes it to himself to conduct an investigation into the roots of the Christian message, if only to be sure his unbelief is not itself unfounded prejudice.[3]

It would be foolish and unrealistic to argue that all Christians hold a faith that is intellectually respectable and based on fact. As with every other system in the world, religious or otherwise, there are immature people in the church who don't give much thought to what they believe and who base their theology on feeling and illogical thinking. Freud, and a host of others, have thrown out Christianity on the basis of their contacts with immature Christians. This is not only unfair, but it is unscientific and unscholarly. Because they think Christianity is stress-producing and for imbeciles, many people turn away from the only power that brings a lasting reduction in stress.

It Isn't Any Fun and It Doesn't Work

Have you ever noticed how many of us like to criticize things we don't really understand? I suspect all of us are guilty of this to at least some extent. Certainly this is true of those who criticize Christianity for its supposed ban on pleasure and its inability to practice what it teaches.

Let's recognize first that the Bible condemns some of the very things which people are enjoying today—excessive drinking, sex outside marriage, and focusing our minds on pornography and other immoral thoughts. The Bible uses the unpopular word "sin" to describe such practices as well as any other behavior or thinking which deviates from the standards of God. While sin is fun (why would people bother with it otherwise?), it is also highly destructive and ultimately creates more stress than it ever solves.

God, in the Person of His Holy Spirit, lives in the life of each believer and gives us the ability to steer clear of sin. We don't always succeed, of course. Christians ignore God's leading and fall into sin too, but we realize that once we confess our sins they are forgiven and that God gives us the power to go on without guilt or tension. And the resulting inner peace spills over into our outward behavior too.

I would be the first to acknowledge that there are many self-centered sourpuss Christians in the world (just like there are miserable nonbelievers). When believers set up a lot of rules to follow or spend no personal time in prayer with God, little wonder they are unhappy. Their religion *has* become a stress. But it need not be that way.

Millions of people have discovered that it is possible to be a dedicated follower of Christ and to thoroughly enjoy life. This is not a fad; it's a conclusion backed up by centuries of history. When people refuse to try it, however, or sit aloof with a critical attitude, they can never know from personal experience that it works!

STRESS AND THE RELIGIOUS LEADER

Until very recently the religious leader—perhaps you prefer the term pastor, minister, or clergyman—held a place of high status even in the eyes of the people outside the church. While this is now changing, many church leaders still enjoy considerable prestige, at least among believers, but this is one reason why the ministry can be a very stressful position.

Consider, for example, the minister's self-concept. Everyone expects the minister to be more spiritual than the rest of the congregation. He (or she) is supposed to have answers to all theological questions and to be a model Christian with a dedicated, well-behaved family. If the parsonage is near the church, everybody can look into the minister's "glass house," and family privacy disappears. It is easy, therefore, for ministers to conclude "I'll never make it, I can't handle the stress." So they shift to other, less demanding (and more lucrative) jobs.[4]

Jobs outside the church may also have a clearer job description. One minister recently polled the 28 officers in his church, asking them what they expected of him and how much time he should spend on activities such as sermon preparation, counseling, visiting the sick, etc. Eighteen of the 28 questionnaires expected the pastor to work more than 100 hours a week, and the average was 136.5 hours![5] If this man met the expectations of his people, he would have only 31.5 hours to himself all week, and if he used all of that time up in sleeping, he'd get 4.5 hours per night. No wonder ministers feel stress! It can come from the very people in his own congregation who pay him, in many cases, far less than they earn themselves in 35- and 40-hour-a-week jobs.

It is difficult for a minister to know if he or she is succeeding. The hours are long, the pay is bad, the demands are great both on the minister and the family, and working conditions are frequently poor. In addition, research studies show that many ministers feel inadequate and ineffective in their work and are not doing what they were trained to do.

Happily, such a bleak and stressful picture does not hold for all clergymen. Many love their work and find it to be immensely fulfilling, but even these people will acknowledge that the job has great stresses—stresses which both the minister and the congregation can work to reduce.

Several years ago I wrote an article on stress in the ministry and submitted it to a denominational magazine for publication. "We are sorry that we cannot publish your article," the editor wrote back. "It deals too much with problems and we feel this shouldn't be in the magazine."[6]

To put it mildly, I was astounded. The worst way to deal with personal problems is to ignore them in hopes that they will go away. They don't go away. Instead, they fester beneath the surface of our awareness, and at a time least expected they explode upon us, sometimes overwhelming us so that our efficiency is impaired and our inner stability is undermined. It accomplishes nothing to conclude, as some do, that "the real Christian shouldn't have problems." Jesus had them, and so did Paul, but they hit the problems head-on.

Certainly this is true in the ministry, where the first question for the church leader to ask is, "Why am I here?" The Christian is likely to ask further, "Is this where God wants me to be?" If so, there can be an inner peace and a willingness to do the best job possible, recognizing that pastors are people too—with imperfections, errors in judgment, limitations, and personalities that grate on some people. If the church leader can't answer these two questions, then it is important to take the time to find answers. Otherwise there will be continuing dissatisfaction and an inner urge to find something better.

A second issue concerns the clergyman's job description. This is the question of "What am I supposed to be doing in this work?" The laymen can help the pastor to mold a clearly written, explicit job description. There may be no single other thing that can do as much to relieve stress in the ministry. Such a task will point to the fact that laymen have specific duties in the church too. The job description should include details of the number of hours that the pastor is normally expected to work, vacation periods, lines of authority in the church or denomination, etc. Remember, no one person can or should try to do everything.

Peter Drucker, the management and efficiency expert, has argued that wasted time is one of the biggest problems in any kind of organization, including the church. To cope with this, Drucker suggests that we should 1) keep a record of where our time is going so we can manage it better; 2) keep in mind a clear idea of what we expect to accomplish in terms of results; 3) build on our own strengths and the strengths of others; and 4) concentrate and work on a few fundamental, major issues.[7]

The Parable of the Garden Hose

Have you ever had a garden hose which leaks in so many places that there is almost nothing coming out of the nozzle? A lot of people's lives are like that. They have an aim in life, but there are so many side interests that they have no power or energy left to give major attention to the top-priority goals. Many ministers are like that. Their goal may be to win people to Jesus Christ, to minister to believers and to help them grow. But committee meetings, church janitorial work, administration, and numerous other activities drain off energy, and the main purpose of the church doesn't get accomplished.

This is not limited to pastors. It applies to housewives, businessmen, professional people, and even writers. After hearing me talk about this, my wife once bought me a very special Christmas present. It is a cartoon of a very perplexed-looking Gary Collins holding a leaky hose with nothing coming out of the nozzle. It is a poignant reminder of the stress-producing tendency to get involved in so many important things that we have no time or energy left for our main goal or goals in life. The cartoon occupies an important place in my study.

Getting Away

There comes a time when all of us should get away from our daily routine. This includes time for "goofing off" with the family, communicating with one's spouse, talking things over with a trusted friend, getting some exercise, and allowing sufficient time for sleep. These are very obvious, of course, but they are stated here because they are so much ignored, especially by pastors, who often pride themselves on a long workweek (and feel guilty when they cut back).

Relaxation relieves stress and enables us to cope more effectively with the pressures of our busy jobs.

STRESS AND THE WORK OF MISSIONS

Being a missionary isn't easy! I've been hearing and reading about this for a long time, but it hit me with greatest clarity when I first visited the mission field several years ago. In traveling from country to country I talked with a variety of experienced missionaries about the stresses of their work and the pressures of serving Christ in a foreign culture.

The pressures varied, I discovered, in several ways. For instance, *the type* of missionary service mattered. Church planting, teaching in a seminary, working in a hospital, or ministering to servicemen overseas each present unique challenges.

The place is important. Some environments are hostile, while others are more open. Some countries present difficult language or cultural barriers. Others are English-speaking and Western in their orientation.

The missionary himself is a unique factor. Personality, marital status, age, experience, and type of training are all variables relevant to the stress one encounters.

The policies of the mission, the effectiveness of the home office, and the expectations from home are also possible sources of pressure on the missionary.

In spite of the differences, some stresses are very common:

Loneliness
The pressures of adjusting to a foreign culture
The constant demands on one's time
The lack of adequate medical facilities
The overwhelming work load and difficult working conditions
Pressure to be a constant, positive "witness" to the nationals
Confusion over one's role within the local church
The frequent lack of privacy
The inability to get away for recreation and vacation.

Most missionaries are creative people who have leadership abilities and the independent spirit which caused them to take the risk of going to the mission field in the first place. Because they must live in close proximity, some of these people become prone to rub against each other in a way that creates tension and increases the potential for conflict. Tired and under pressure, these missionaries can feel tense, critical, or unable to get along with people. It is easy to feel physically, emotionally, and spiritually drained, all of which contribute to inefficiency and further frustration.

Perhaps one of the greatest stresses that missionaries face is guilt. The home church often treats the missionary as if he or she is the most superspiritual of all Christians. Such an ideal is difficult to maintain, especially when the people back home are expecting prayer letters with glowing reports of heathen masses turning to Christ. Even on the field, the missionary often feels compelled to keep up a high spiritual image. To admit one's weaknesses and frustrations might be to imply that one is a poor Christian, perhaps not even worthy to be a missionary. The result can be a phony spirituality accompanied by more guilt. In addition, guilt can come from failure to answer letters, using one's salary (which has been given to the Lord's work by the Lord's people) to buy clothes or go out for dinner. Driving a newer car than the folks back home or the nationals on the field, sending one's children away to a missionary school, leaving aged parents at home, taking time to relax, or not meeting the expectations of one's supporters may also lead to guilt. Such guilt leads to frustration or anger, and that creates more stress.

It should not be assumed, of course, that the missionary's life is all pressure and stress. There are innumerable rewards in missionary service, and by acknowledging the difficulties we are able to avoid some of the pressures which otherwise might hinder the missionary's effectiveness. There are three main areas where the Christian church can help to reduce missionary stress.

Three Ways to Help

First, there is the area of *preparation*. We need to select and train missionaries more carefully, recognizing that a "felt call," a psychological screening, and the approval of mission executives are not sufficient for the choosing of candidates for the field. Perhaps veteran missionaries need to be involved in selection. In addition, on-the-job training at home, giving an accurate picture of the field of service, and some training in how to cope with stress should all be part of the missionary's preparation. There needs to be more research in how to select and train good missionaries. This is a better use of the church's resources than to send out missionaries to fend for themselves, to learn by experience, and sometimes to fail, with the resulting loss of face among supporters back home.

Communication is basic to facing stress and getting along with people. Whether or not they are missionaries, Christians must learn to get along with each other. They must learn to communicate with their spouses, to talk to nonbelievers, to fellowship with God. They must be ready to bear one another's burdens, to weep with those who weep, and to rejoice with those who rejoice. This involves skill and training in interpersonal relations. It is needed by Christians at home and abroad, but is seems to be lacking among many believers today. Because of this inability to communicate, we experience and are overpowered by much more stress than is necessary. This certainly applies to the mission field, where communication skill is essential, especially between co-workers.

Finally, there is *expectation*. We must quit expecting the missionary to be a perfect model of efficiency and spirituality. Missionaries are people who need prayer, encouragement, and understanding. By relieving some of the pressure from home the missionary is better equipped to handle the less-avoidable stresses on the field.

As we have seen, stress isn't all bad. It can stretch us, motivate us, and cause us to grow. When stress gets too intense, however, it can stifle and hinder a ministry. The key to success is reducing the pressure to a point where it motivates without immobilizing. Better preparation, the development of communication skills, and the demonstration of realistic expectations are key steps to reducing missionary stress.[8]

STRESS IN THE LOCAL CHURCH

In his letters to the young churches in New Testament times, Paul often mentioned the quarrels that were frequently taking place between the believers. The same struggles are described in the Book of Acts, and in the two thousand years since that time things haven't changed much.

Not long ago the police were called one Sunday morning to the steps of a church which had divided into two factions. Each side wanted access to the building but was refusing to let the other side in. Because of the squabble, a judge had closed the church for a three-week "cooling-off period," and in the meantime the newspapers had great fun pointing to the lack of unity among those who called themselves brethren.

Very often these disputes are over silly things or center around personalities with giant ego problems. Regardless of the causes, however, stress in the church leads to (and follows from) stress in the church members. To meet such stresses it would seem that churches need to be both Christ-centered and deeply concerned about the personal growth within the congregation.

Christ-Centered Churches

When there is tension between people in the church, it is often true that Christ is not at the center of the congregation. He breaks down the walls that divide people,[9] so that when walls persist it is logical to conclude that Christ isn't in control. What is in control, very often, is somebody's personal opinion or "reputation." Dishonesty, insensitivity, a lack of concern for others, and rigidity often follow as the factions develop.

How have churches drifted into this kind of stress-producing division? The answer may be that we have deviated from the Biblical guidelines for churches and have instead created big buildings which sit empty for most of the week, superstar pastors who run a big organization, and passive congregations who come to be preached at and entertained. This is neither good psychology nor good theology.

In a thought-provoking and controversial book, missionary educator Howard Snyder makes some interesting observations about church structure: "It is hard to escape the conclusion," Snyder writes in the first chapter of his book, "that today one of the greatest roadblocks to the gospel of Jesus Christ is the institutional church."[10]

Snyder does not deny the importance of large services where many people come together for worship. But, he maintains, if there is to be vitality in the church there must be small groups which meet regularly to study the Bible and to communicate both with God and with each other. Such groups can have tremendous stress-reducing potential, especially if they focus more on Christ than on church politics or on the empire-building schemes of one or two church leaders.

High Walls and Personal Growth

There are several basic principles for breaking down the walls between us and getting along with each other. These are principles which apply outside the church as well as within.

It is important, for example, that we learn to listen and attempt to understand the other person's point of view. We should be honest, expressing what we think or feel but being careful to speak the truth with love and a sensitivity to the other person's feelings. We should do what we can to compromise, to discuss differences carefully, and to fight against self-pity, jealousy, revenge-taking, or relying on feelings alone. All of this is difficult because it seemingly goes against our basic nature and it means taking a risk. Openness, like we are suggesting, makes us vulnerable to the attacks of others, but ultimately this creates less stress than the hiding of feelings and the dishonesty that typifies so many of our contacts with others today.

When we build walls around ourselves or around our church denomination, we might feel protected but we cannot reach out to others, and there is no opportunity for personal growth. I remember once passing a church in London named "The Strict and Particular Baptist Church." No doubt the members were dedicated to the lofty goal of separation from worldliness, but I wonder if that church was also obsolete, rigidified, self-centered, and in such a binding, self-created straitjacket that it was unable to reach out to fulfill the Great Commission.

The church today, as always, must be Christ-centered and built on the Scriptures. But it must also be people-directed, set on the task of supporting, encouraging, and training stress-prone believers so they can reach out to a stress-saturated world with the liberating good news of Jesus Christ.

Part Three

HANDLING STRESS:

Permanent Coping

Chapter 12
ESCAPING FROM STRESS

As every author knows, writing a book can be an intense, exhaustive task. It requires discipline, persistence, and (at least for me) a willingness to keep going even when I don't feel very inspired or enthused about what has been written.

One way to keep my mind clear is to take frequent breaks. It has been estimated that the average span of concentration for most adults is about 1 ½ hours, so after sitting for roughly that length of time I take a minibreak, stretching my muscles, walking around the room, and skimming what has been written thus far.

Perhaps the time has come for us to take a minibreak in this book to see where we have been and to look at where we are going. In Part One of the book we tried to lay a foundation for understanding and dealing with stress. We looked at the meaning of stress, considered its effects and origins, and laid down some general guidelines for coping. Part Two of the book has dealt with stress in our daily lives—our families, our jobs, our life crises, and our religion.

We now come to some of the ways in which people attempt to handle stress on a more permanent basis. Each of the methods described in the next two chapters has an enthusiastic band of advocates. In this chapter we will try to look at the most-widely-used methods for escaping stress, and in the next chapter we will give a number of proven techniques that you can try in your own life.

THE SEARCH FOR TRANQUILITY

"Transpersonal psychology" is the name of a small but growing movement which seeks to find self-fulfillment, inner peace, and stability either by probing into outer space, looking for some kind of a deity, or looking within ourselves. In America alone there are currently over eight thousand systems for "psychospiritual growth."[1] Some are simple, others are complex. Some involve great sacrifice and personal discipline while others are easy. Some promise sure success while others make less exorbitant claims. All of these approaches have one thing in common, however: they each offer the promise of personal growth and a greater ability to cope with the stresses of life.

Some of these approaches are embarrassed by enthusiastic and sometimes growing bands of followers, but at least for the present they wouldn't be considered major social movements. Examples include Silva Mind Control, Self-Realization, Subud, Hasidism, the Rosicrucians, Vedanta, Sufism, Zen Buddhism, Psychosynthesis, the Hare Krishna Movement, and something called 3HO (the Healthy, Happy, Holy Organization).[2] Other movements, like yoga, encounter groups, and EST, seem to be growing at a faster rate and attracting increasing popular attention.

In this chapter we will not try to discuss all of these movements. That would be both futile and boring. Instead, we will focus our attention on four of the best-known techniques for relieving stress: drugs (the most available), biofeedback (the most scientific), hypnosis (the most psychological), and meditation (currently the most popular).

HIDING YOUR TENSIONS WITH DRUGS

Drugs have been used for centuries to dull pain, create a sense of well-being, and sometimes help people with their religious experiences. It was early in the 1950's, however, when the so-called psychotropic drugs hit the market and almost overnight revolutionized modern society. These drugs calmed people down without dulling the brain or hindering their ability to engage in daily activities. Very quickly, mental hospitals became quiet, people who otherwise might be overwhelmed with stress found that they could get along, and drug sales began booming. It was discovered that drugs, many of which were available without a prescription, could be used to reduce anxiety, combat depression, relieve or prevent fatigue, create a sense of self-confidence, take away tension, eliminate insomnia, reduce hostility or agitation, relieve boredom, and sometimes produce euphoria. Medical journals have warned against the "drugging of America," but the use and abuse of both legal and illegal drugs has become a part of our way of life.

It is easy to read the above paragraph and shake our heads in dismay while failing to recognize that almost all of us are involved to some extent. Pills to keep us awake, to help us sleep, to lose weight, and even to reduce stress are widely available and are as common in many households as the aspirin which fights colds, the caffeine-saturated cola which the kids drink for refreshment, and the coffee which we use to wake up in the morning.

In themselves, drugs are not bad. On the contrary, they have had a marvelous influence in relieving pain, preventing infection, curing disease, and helping disturbed people cope with life's pressures. It has become apparent, however, that drugs can be misused and in the long run can become more harmful than helpful.

It must be recognized, for example, that while medicine can effectively combat disease, stress-relieving drugs never solve anything; they only obscure problems. Is it wise, somebody has asked, to make ourselves feel secure when we are really in danger, to feel happy when there is reason to grieve, to experience a surge of energy when our bodies are fatigued and in need of sleep? Isn't it more likely that we will correct a situation if we are disturbed by it? Christians have worked on this assumption for years; we don't spend much time getting into a right relationship with God if well-meaning but misinformed preachers lull us into believing that man is innately good and has no need of a Savior. Some sense of urgency impels us to action. Drugs dull that sense of urgency.

This is not to deny, however, that for many people the stress in their lives is so great that without the calming effect of medication they could not think clearly enough to handle their problems or sit still long enough to discuss them with a counselor. If drugs help us to control our anxieties temporarily, they serve a useful purpose. If they prevent us from facing our stresses and simply obscure our problems, then drugs are being misused.

There is another problem with the use of drugs. Even when they are not *physiologically* addictive, their use becomes *psychologically* habit-forming, so that people become dependent on them. If pills help you through a crisis, fine, but if you rely on them day after day, you begin to feel you can't do without them. The more we rely on drugs the less able we are to handle stress without them; we become slaves to various medications, and by our own actions we contribute to the drugging of America.

There is evidence, incidentally, that this pill-taking becomes an example for children and teenagers, who are less perceptive than adults about which drugs are harmful. "Dad and Mom use pills to solve their problems," the young person might think, "so why shouldn't I?"

The Most Common Drug of All

The most common drug of all is not Librium, Valium, Miltown, Tofrinil, Phenobarbital, or even No-Doz, Compoz and Excedrin. The most widely used drug in America and abroad is alcohol. An estimated 71 percent of the American population drinks at least occasionally, and of these nearly nine million are alcoholics. (However, most people who drink, even to relieve stress and "unwind" over a cocktail, do not become alcoholics.)

There are various theories as to why people drink excessively, but an attempt to find relief from stress seems to be basic. Alcoholism stems from psychological needs, writes one physician.[3] It "is used to deal with insecurity, anxiety, depression, or stress. These conditions may be relieved by other means, but some people seem to find alcohol peculiarly effective." At first the drinking is social and gives a sense of relaxation and well-being. Later, alcohol becomes an escape from stress or feelings of inadequacy, and then, as the need for alcohol increases, the drinker's self-control lessens. That which began as an *escape* from stress became a major *cause* of stress in the drinkers and their families.

In her book for the families and employers of problem drinkers,[4] Ruth Maxwell estimates that more than 36 million people in the United States alone (roughly one-sixth of the population) are directly affected by drinking relatives or friends. When a family member drinks excessively the whole family stability is shaken. There are scenes of drunken behavior accompanied by arguments, promises to reform, denials of the problem, and family attempts to hide the excessive drinking from the outside world.

There are distinct stages in alcohol addiction, stages which the drinker might deny but the family can easily see.[5] Near the beginning there is a preoccupation with drinking and a great concern about whether there is enough liquor available or whether there will be enough at a party. Then there are blackouts, periods of amnesia during which the drinker does things he cannot remember later. Loss of control comes next. The drinker may have rules about when and where he will drink, but he soon breaks those rules, and one drink seems to trigger a chain of drinking which ends in drunkenness. Soon the problem drinker begins to drink alone, and then he or she experiences intense hangovers which are sometimes "treated" by morning drinks, and before long drinking becomes an obsession. Even at this point the drinker may attempt to deny his or her problem. Such a person needs help, and so does the family.

Dealing with Alcoholism

There are a variety of treatment techniques for alcoholism. Christians recognize and utilize the power of prayer, and we know that God in His wisdom sometimes intervenes directly to bring change. Frequently, however, God answers prayer by leading us to counselors and other human resources for treatment.

Undoubtedly the most effective of these include Alcoholics Anonymous (AA), Al-Anon (the support group for spouses), and Alateen, a group for teenage relatives of alcoholics.[6] In their attempts to deny the problem, drinkers are very effective in manipulating their families. The families, in turn, fail to realize that their patient and persistent attempts to reform a drinker only accentuate the problem and make it worse. Families and employers can be the key influence in getting the alcoholic into treatment, but according to one expert in the field this won't be done by persuasion, coercion, pleading, threatening, or "covering up" for the drinker. It is better to make contact with an AA group for support and help, to attempt to live as normal a life as possible (but without the alcoholic's involvement in social gatherings), to be open about the problem with others, and to be sensitive to the drinker's needs while continuing to remind him or her of the behavior that comes with drinking. One woman reminded her husband that he had parked his car on a neighbor's lawn the night before. When the husband denied this, the wife informed him that she hadn't bothered to move it. It is this confrontation with evidence that lets the drinker see that he has to face his behavior and do something about it. His family must not be manipulated into hiding the problem.[7]

At first this sounds cruel, but it may be the only way to get the alcoholic to recognize his or her need for help. Once he or she goes for help—perhaps to AA, to a counselor, or to a treatment center—then the problem can be cured, especially if the drinker learns better ways to deal with the stresses of life.

CALMING YOUR BODY THROUGH BIOFEEDBACK

The great Houdini used to do escape tricks in which he first would be thoroughly searched to make sure he was concealing no keys, and then he would allow himself to be locked in chains, padlocks, and handcuffs. Of course not even Houdini could open a lock without a key, but when out of sight he would literally cough one up. He had the ability to hold a key suspended in his throat until he needed it to undo the locks.

When you think about it, this was an amazing feat. Ordinarily, when an object is stuck in the throat, we gag, but Houdini had learned to control his gag reflex by practicing for hours with a small piece of potato tied to a string.

In doing this, Houdini (and a few eastern Yogis) had discovered something that has recently become a breakthrough in modern science. We can, with a little effort, voluntarily control those parts and functions of the body which we once thought were uncontrollable. Laboratory studies have demonstrated that we can control the heartbeat, the temperature of the skin, the flow of blood, the muscles that produce headaches, high blood pressure (hypertension), the contracted muscles that make us feel tense or which lead to a variety of psychosomatic diseases, and the electrical voltage in the brain.[8]

Back in the 1920's, a psychiatrist named Hans Berger discovered in his German laboratory that the brain emits electrical signals which can be measured by a sensitive recording machine which has since been called the electroencephalograph (or EEG). There are, according to Berger, four types of brain signals, each of which has been identified with a Greek letter. When the brain is most active—including when we are angry, worried, pressured, or irritable—it gives off high-frequency impulses known as *beta* waves. Next down the scale, when we are relaxed, calm, or more contemplative, are the *alpha* waves. *Theta* conditions come during deep thought, and *delta* waves come when we are asleep. It has been demonstrated conclusively that people can be trained to shift their brain waves from beta to alpha and sometimes even to theta.

The yogis of India and the Eastern mystics have apparently learned such internal self-control through years of quiet meditation and concentration on their bodies. But Westerners are too impatient for that, so we have developed "instant yoga."

This gets us to a description of biofeedback. Let us assume that a person's brainwave patterns can be signaled by a tone, perhaps a loud tone for beta, a quieter tone for alpha, and a still quieter tone for theta. Now the person hears the tone and is told to produce alpha waves. It becomes a tiring experience, but soon the alpha waves come and the subject hears the tones change accordingly. When this is done in laboratories,[9] the subjects are not told how to produce alpha. Most think about peaceful times in the past when they felt contented and happy. It may take as long as ten hours, but by using the tone signals anyone can learn to attain and maintain alpha whenever they want. The same training can help us relax muscles, eliminate tension headaches, slow our heartbeat, and quickly relax— whenever we want to.

Regretfully, all of this training involves the use of expensive machines. Within recent years biofeedback machines for home use have appeared on the market, but as yet they aren't very effective. I am reminded, however, of the response of one apparently skeptical medical researcher. Through the use of biofeedback machines he had seen blood pressure drop, but when asked how they did it, the subjects replied that they simply thought relaxing thoughts. "If that is so," my medical friend concluded, "why not just think the thoughts and forget the machines?"

COPING WITH STRESS THROUGH HYPNOSIS

My first real encounter with hypnosis came one summer when I was in an officer training program with the reserve Navy. Over dinner one night a fellow trainee happened to mention that he had taken clinical training in hypnotism, and this led six or seven of us to move into a sideroom for a demonstration. I was the first subject, but I felt so silly that I started to giggle (which is something I never do otherwise), and so I didn't do much to prove the hypnotist's powers. There were other people in the room, however, who were less of a problem for the hypnotist. Whenever he began talking, the eyes of an older lieutenant-commander would close and his head would flop forward in what appeared to be deep sleep.

In its 200-year history hypnosis has been studied by a variety of researchers. These experimenters have found, as I discovered that night in the Navy, that there are great individual differences in the ease with which people can be hypnotized. There are differences both in the techniques hypnotists use and in the physiological changes of the hypnotized person. In addition, there are also a number of myths about hypnosis, myths which lead people to think that this is a powerful technique capable of solving a great variety of problems.

It is more accurate to conclude that hypnosis is primarily a state of intense concentration in which the person is highly suggestible. Consider, for example, how the hypnotist usually works. He or she encourages the subject to relax and focus attention on some object. Then there is a monotonous repetition of suggestions, often accompanied by the building of an emotional relationship between the hypnotist and the subject. Hypnotism does not involve sleep (even though subjects are often told that they will fall into a "deep sleep"); it is not a wierd, mysterious experience; it apparently is not a state in which you can be persuaded to do immoral or criminal acts; and it is not something from which you will never wake up. Very often the subject is told to look up and focus on a dangling pendant or pencil tip. Naturally this tires the eye muscles, and the eyelids are inclined to close. When the hypnotist drones, "You are getting very tired," we begin to agree and assume that someone else's power is at work. If he says, "Your eyes are stuck shut," we might think, "That's probably not true, but I don't feel like opening them, so I'll keep him happy by leaving them shut." In spite of these inner rationalizations your eyes remain closed.

You also feel relaxed, and that's what makes hypnosis a popular technique for handling stress. It is a technique which has become even more important with the realization that we can easily hypnotize ourselves. There are probably hundreds of ways to do this, but in every case there is a self-disciplined focusing of attention on some subject.

I used to do this when I was a graduate student pressured with deadlines and assignments. I would lay in a relaxed state, close my eyes, and think about a tree stump that was near the university. I'd tell myself, "You are getting very tired thinking about the tree stump. Think of nothing else but the tree stump." And soon I'd be relaxed if not asleep. I didn't know it at the time, but I could have said things like, "You are relaxing. You are forgetting all your exciting work and pressing deadlines. Your body is completely relaxed." In this age of technology one writer has even suggested that we record such suggestions on a tape recorder and listen to ourselves when we want to relax.

There are some problems with all of the self-centered behavior. In the first place, nobody knows for sure what hypnosis is or why it works. It does bring a sense of relaxation, but do we want to play with something we know so little about? In addition, the use of hypnosis can be like a stress-relieving drug. It can relax us without dealing with life's problems. And there is one other thing to note. Hypnosis isn't necessary. Freud concluded this almost a century ago, and more recent research (which is admittedly controversial) has shown that all the benefits that are supposed to come from a hypnotic trance can come without the trance, by self-suggestion or the suggestion of another person.[10]

RELAXATION THROUGH MEDITATION

Maharishi Mahesh Yogi is, to put it mildly, an interesting individual. Son of a forest ranger, the Maharishi (the word means Great Seer in Sanskrit) is said to have graduated from Allahabad University before coming under the religious influence of Guru Dev (which means "Divine Leader"). For thirteen years the two men were together, and before his death Guru Dev charged the Maharishi with the mission of making meditation simple enough to be practiced by anybody. For two years while living alone in the Himalayas the Maharishi worked on this task, and then, in the mid-1950's, he launched the Transcendental Meditation (TM) movement.

The TM movement first gained public attention when the Beatles went to the Maharishi's residence in India, where they took up TM as an alternative to using drugs. A stream of show-business people followed, and soon the Maharishi was big news. In the United States alone roughly three quarters of a million people have been taught TM, and the Maharishi has addressed state legislatures, appeared on TV talk shows, traveled with rock groups, and established Maharishi International University, which trains students to spread the message of TM. His message has spread to cities and especially college towns all over the world, and the movement is still growing.

Perhaps it's the Maharishi's quiet manner that made him attractive. Maybe it is the American (or perhaps human) tendency to always be looking for something new and different. Undoubtedly, however, Transcendental Meditation really caught on when it was discovered that this technique could quickly and effectively alleviate many of the stress symptoms that so plague our hectic-paced society.

For several years a Harvard cardiologist named Herbert Benson and physiologist Robert Keith Wallace have studied the physiological effects of meditation. The results have been dramatic. Blood pressure drops, the heartbeat slows, there is an increase in alpha waves in the brain, breathing slows, and the subjects report an internal sense of relaxation.[11] While there are some technical problems with this research, it is nevertheless impressive.

In another study, nonmeditators were compared with meditators in their reaction to a stressful movie. The meditators handled the stress much better. Their heartbeat returned to normal more quickly, and physiological measures showed that they adjusted to the poststress situation more easily.[12]

TM and Religion

In spite of the Maharishi's Hindu background, the advocates of TM insist that this is a purely scientific technique for reducing stress and is not a religious movement. However, there is considerable evidence to refute this claim.[13]

Consider, for example, the mantra. This is a Sanskrit work given by an instructor to the meditator to be repeated over and over again for twenty minutes every morning and evening. According to the Maharishi, in meditation "we do something . . . according to the Vedic rites, particularly, specific chanting to produce an effect in some other world, draw the attention of those higher beings or gods living there."[14]

The religious aspect of TM comes out even more clearly in some of the Maharishi's other statements:

Transcendental Meditation is a path to God.[15]

A very good form of prayer is this meditation which leads to the field of the creator, to the source of creation, to the field of God.[16]

[Transcendental Meditation] is the only way to salvation and successes in life; there is no other way.[17]

Even more indicative of Hinduism is the initiation ceremony, in which all potential candidates are required to participate. The candidate is asked to bring some flowers, three pieces of fruit, and a handkerchief, all of which are placed before a picture of Guru Dev, Maharishi's departed Master. The room is candlelit and incense fills the air as the TM teacher sings a ritual hymn of thanksgiving. After the song, the student is instructed to kneel for a few minutes with the teacher, and then the candidate is told his mantra and asked to repeat it.

Modern people often feel a little silly about this ritual, but they quickly forget their objections when they begin to experience the relaxation that follows. A recently obtained English translation of the "song of thanksgiving" shows that this is a hymn of worship in which the words "I bow down" occur several times. Because the chant is in Sanskrit, the TM initiate doesn't even realize that he or she is participating in a Hindu worship ceremony with a chant that says, in part:

> To Lord Narayana, to lotus-born Brahma, the Creator . . . I
>   bow down . . . .
> To Shankara, emancipator of the world, I bow down.
> To Shakaracharya, the redeemer . . . I bow down. . . .
> To Shri Guru Dev adorned with glory, I bow down.[18]

TM clearly helps people to relieve stress, but to do so the mediator engages in a Hindu religion which masquerades as science.

No Christian, therefore, can be involved in TM. It is absolutely at odds with the teachings of the Bible, in which we are instructed repeatedly to have no deities other than the Lord God of the Scriptures.[19]

Meditation Without TM

Might it be possible for us to eliminate the religious aspects of TM and meditate without the Hinduism? Dr. Herbert Benson, the Harvard researcher, thinks so, and in his bestselling book *The Relaxation Response*[20] he tells how this can be done.

There isn't much we can do to change the complex, stress-producing pace of modern life, Dr. Benson maintains, but we can learn ways to cope with it more effectively. TM is one of these ways, but it isn't the only one, nor is it particularly new or unique.

For centuries people have learned to relax, and if we look at all the different approaches, religious and otherwise, we discover four common elements. First, there must be a quiet environment with as few distractions as possible. Second, there must be an object to dwell on. This may be a word, a sound, a mental image—anything which can keep the mind from wandering and can clear away distracting thoughts. TM uses a mantra; Dr. Benson uses the word "one." Every time you breathe out you say the word "one."

The third element in all meditation is a passive attitude. This is very important, according to Dr. Benson's research. Thoughts and distractions are certain to come, but the meditator ignores them and keeps thinking of the mental object. No thought should be given to questions like, "Am I doing it correctly?" or "Is this how people meditate?"

Finally, there must be a comfortable position, one which you can maintain for twenty minutes.

Does this work as well as TM? According to Dr. Benson it does, and he can demonstrate this with his studies of lowered blood pressure and decreasing use of drugs, lowered oxygen consumption and lowered blood-lactate levels—all of which indicate less anxiety as a result of using the "relaxation response" approach to meditation.

THE PROBLEM WITH ESCAPING

Do you remember several years ago, when a drug named thalidomide hit the market in Europe? It was supposed to eliminate the symptoms of morning sickness in pregnant women, but it did something else as well. Hundreds of mothers who had taken the drug discovered too late that they had given birth to infants whose arms and legs had not developed. Here was a situation in which a cure for the stressful symptoms of morning sickness turned out to be worse than the discomfort.

In writing this chapter I have had the distinct impression that for many of the escape techniques the cure may turn out to be worse than the stress from which we are trying to escape!

The escape techniques tend to assume that stress is bad and should be eliminated. Stress is damaging physically and psychologically, but might it also be alerting us to certain things which need to be corrected? Stress researcher Hans Selye has argued that without some stress we would die, and he maintains that *excessive* stress, what he calls distress, is what we really want to eliminate.[21]

While this may be playing with words, the fact remains that complete relaxation hides the causes of our stress but does nothing about them. We can be lulled or drugged into a state of inactivity, which prevents our tackling the basic reasons which cause the stress in the first place.

Improper escape techniques can dull our thinking and open our minds to harmful influences. We know that alcohol dulls thinking, and now there is evidence that TM may decrease our ability to think creatively.[22]

The Bible never approves of passive meditation or clearing the mind. On the contrary, a dull mind is condemned, and we are commanded instead to be sober and on the alert, actively resisting the schemes of the Devil.[23] The Bible even says something about meditation. This is to be done daily and must put our focus on the Bible, the Word of God. Meditation is not to involve the vain repetition of a mantra or a word like "one." That is a heathen practice.[24] Only a meditation on the Word of God is acceptable in God's sight. It is this which puts us in touch with the real source of peace for mankind, the Prince of Peace, Jesus Christ.

Improper escape techniques elevate man and deny the need for any experience with God. The fundamental assumption of Eastern religion and Western humanism is that man is autonomous, good, and the closest thing there is to a deity. By attempting to solve our stress problems by ourselves we demonstrate to the world and to ourselves that we think God is unnecessary and perhaps even nonexistent. One TM leader put it this way: "I noticed as I began meditating more and more a growing pride and insensitivity to others—even though I felt more calm and confident than ever before. I realized I was becoming, in fact, my own god."[25]

God has permitted mankind to discover a number of techniques for dealing with physical and mental stresses. But when these are used to glorify man and ignore God, they are being misused to man's own ultimate destruction. The Bible states clearly that man on his own cannot cope with the stresses of this life and the next.[26] Improper escape techniques often present the exact opposite conclusions.

Improper escape techniques desensitize the conscience and promise happiness without facing the issue of sin. Sin is not a popular word anymore, and moderns like to pretend it is an outdated concept. Listen, for example, to the Maharishi. Through TM "very easily a sinner comes out of the field of sin and becomes a virtuous man." Now listen to the Bible: "All have sinned and this leads to death, but the free gift of God is eternal life in Christ Jesus our Lord."[27]

The stress-saturated world in which we live has produced a number of devices for dealing with life's pressures. Many of these are clearly effective in reducing stress and changing the physiological reactions which accompany stress and harm our bodies. Before we accept these escape techniques, however, we had better look for hidden dangers and faulty assumptions which may indicate that some of the proposed cures for stress are really worse than the disease.

Chapter 13
WINNING OVER STRESS

In 1929 a Chicago physician named Edmund Jacobson wrote a book to outline something which he called "progressive relaxation." It was a technical book and was so difficult to understand that the doctor later wrote a layman's edition titled simply *You Must Relax*.[1] The New York *Post* called it a "priceless little book" and the Chicago *Tribune* predicted that "many lives will undoubtedly be saved by Dr. Jacobson's little volume, for in a simple and practical way he reveals the secret of 'taking it easy' and at the same time getting one's daily work done."

Perhaps this was the beginning of relaxation books, but they have come with increasing frequency, especially during the past ten years. The titles can be intriguing: *Triumph over Tension, Learn to Relax, Stress Without Distress, Escape from Stress, How to Handle Pressure, The Relaxation Response*, to name a few. That books like these (and the one you are reading) continue to appear must indicate that many people still have not learned to relax or to profit from stress.

LEARNING TO COPE

There are proven techniques that can enable us to cope successfully without dulling our minds, decreasing our efficiency, or selling ourselves to non-Christian philosophies. Some of these techniques are simple, so much so that they are often overlooked or dismissed as unimportant. Consider, for example, the following list[2] of stress-reducing suggestions, each of which is very basic and each of which works:

—Don't play roles. Trying to be the "liberated woman" or the "cool businessman," for example, will only create stress because you are not being yourself.

—Choose your friends wisely. Seek people who are pleasant to be with, and where possible avoid contact with those who criticize or tear you down. Remember that you become like the people with whom you associate.

—Don't let things drift. If there is unhappiness or worry in your life, try to do something about the problem. Procrastination and indecision only delay your misery.

—Admit your fears. Find out what scares you and try to determine why. Discuss this with a friend if necessary.

—Make time to get away. A few minutes of privacy each day, when you can relax and think, is important even for children. Find a way to do this even if it means getting up early or going for a brief walk.

—Do something for others. It's difficult to worry about yourself when you are helping others.

—Be willing to compromise. This is a sign of strength, not weakness. To be rigid, to refuse to give in, or to insist on winning all create tension.

—Work on a realistic self-image. Recognize that you have both strong and weak points. Build on the strong points and excel in these areas. Work at improving the weak areas, but realize that you can't do everything well— nobody can.

—Always do what is right. Cheating, deception, unethical behavior, immorality—these can all produce guilt feelings, self-condemnation, attempts to "cover up," and of course tension. Admit your faults, confess your sins to God, and get into the habit of doing what is right.

—Take one thing at a time. Start with the most important or difficult task and go from there. Make lists, if this helps, and cross things off as they are accomplished.

—Seek a balance in your life—work, leisure, physical exercise, contemplation, and resting are all part of life. You can overdo any of these, just as you can avoid any, and either situation creates stress.

—Be realistic. Recognize that you can change some things but not others.

—Recognize the tension-reducing value in swimming, *relaxing* music, casual reading, and even television. These are diversionary activities, all of which can help when practiced in moderation.

—Slow down. Practice moving more slowly. Slow your speech when you talk and your pace when you walk. Eat with slower movements, putting down your fork between bites. When you move more slowly you feel less pressured.

—Avoid excuses. Blaming other people or circumstances doesn't help much. Take responsibility for yourself and your own actions.

—Talk things over. A friend, relative, pastor, or professional counselor can often help you see things that are unclear otherwise. Don't be afraid to turn to these outside sources for help.

How to Relax

Stress, as we have seen , involves the body's tensing up in an emergency and getting ready for a flight-or-fight action. What often happens in our hurly-burly world is that our bodies are tensed up all the time, with our muscles, heart, and stomach in a constant state of alert. As a result we eventually collapse under the strain.

The best way to attack this problem is by getting to the source of the stress, but there can also be value in dealing with the symptoms. This is what we mean by relaxation—helping the body to get off the alert and resume a more normal rate of functioning. Biofeedback is one way of doing this; doing some relaxation exercises is another.

In Table 3 we have listed several exercises that can help you to relax. These can be done by almost anyone, and they don't need any special equipment or physical skill. These aren't the only answers to winning over stress, but they are a step in the right direction.

━━━ TABLE 3 ━━━
RELAXATION EXERCISES

The following exercises are designed to help relax your muscles. To begin, loosen any belt or other tight clothing and take off your shoes. Then try one or two of the following. Try each of these during the next few days and decide which is most appropriate for you.

MUSCLE RELAXATION

Lie on your back with your arms at your sides. Tense and relax each group of muscles two or three times. Then, as you relax, go on to the next group.

Begin with your toes. Curl them toward the floor, then relax them. Repeat this once or twice.

Now point your toes toward your face as far as possible. Tense your calves, then relax.

Lift your legs until your feet are about a foot from the floor, then tense your thighs and let your legs fall to the floor.

Tense your buttocks and then relax them.

Take a deep breath, hold it for a few seconds, then exhale.

Push your head forward. Touch your chest, then lay your head on the floor again.

Close your eyes tightly. Tighten your lips, screw up your face, and wiggle your forehead. Relax.

Clench your fists tightly. Hold this for five seconds, then loosen your grip.

Spread out your fingers as widely as you can. Then relax.

Touch your shoulders and flex your biceps muscles. Relax.

Shrug your shoulders as if you were trying to touch your ears. Relax.

Repeat the above two or three times wherever you still feel tense.

Lie still for a minute or two and enjoy the relaxed state. Get up slowly, without rushing.

BREATHING

Breathing can do much to stop tension. Lie on the floor with your knees bent slightly. Put one hand on your stomach and the other on your chest. Draw breath into your stomach and feel it rise. Try to keep your chest from moving very much. Breathe in through your nose and out through your mouth. Each time breathe as deeply as you can and say "haaaah" as you exhale. Do this for five or ten minutes.

SIT AND STRETCH

These are exercises you can do while sitting and without anyone knowing what you are doing. One man, a public speaker, does these to relax while sitting on the platform waiting to be introduced.

Wiggle your toes for one or two minutes.
Circle your feet by rotating your ankles.
Tighten your buttocks, count to five, then relax.
Inhale deeply into your abdomen, exhale slowly, then relax.
Stretch your fingers as far apart as possible, then relax.
Squeeze your fists tightly, hold the grip for five seconds, then relax.
Let your hands go limp and dangle your hands loosely from the wrists.
Look up to the ceiling or sky, raising both shoulders as you do.

If you are alone, in addition to the above you can stretch your arms as high into the air as possible and stretch your feet straight out from the seat of the chair. (Don't do this on a public platform or you might not be invited to speak!)

SHOULDER STRETCH

This can be done several times during the day. Drop your head forward to rest on your chest. Now slowly rotate your head to the left as far as possible, lift your shoulder to touch your ear, then tilt your head back as far as you can (so you are looking upward). Next, move your head slowly to the right, touching your shoulder, and then return to the chin-on-chest position. Repeat by rotating your head in the other direction. Breathe naturally, letting your mouth drop open if you wish.

SITTER'S PUSHUPS

While you are seated, put your hands on the arms or seat of your chair and push, lifting your whole body off the chair.

MUSCLE MASSAGE

Massage your tense muscles in the direction of your heart. Massaging your feet or shoulders can be especially relaxing. If you are a speaker or teacher, you might want to massage your throat or neck muscles.

BE A PEOPLE HELPER

Here one person can lie in a relaxed position on the floor or on a bed while another person massages his feet (stroking toward the heart) or rubs his back and shoulder muscles.

An electric vibrator can be purchased for about fifteen dollars and can be used for both back and foot massage.

The Crucial Importance of Leisure

When Hans Selye first published his now-classic book on the stress of life, he made the proposal that "no one part of the body must be disproportionately overworked for a long time."[3] It's like carrying a heavy suitcase; when one arm feels a strain (stress), you shift the bag to the other arm, so that the stress is equalized and no one set of muscles is overworked.

The same is true in life. If we spend almost all our time working, or relaxing, or doing church and community work, then we are overexerting one part of our personality, and this is tension-producing.

As we noted in an earlier chapter, many people today have become workaholics. They spend long hours at work and may thoroughly enjoy what they are doing, but they are not living balanced lives. Eventually nature catches up to them, and because of a heart attack or other physical problem they are forced to slow down.

A better way to start slowing down is with our attitudes. We must recognize that leisure is not wrong or unnecessary and is not a misuse of talent or a waste of time. Even God rested on the seventh day after creation, and He has instructed us to do the same. Leisure is as important to life as work. If we fail to take time for recreation, we may succeed in our vocations but lose our family, friends, and health. Even short breaks, taken frequently, can rejuvenate us and make our work more effective.

Having decided that leisure is important, decide *how* to unwind. That is difficult for some people, but a good place to start is with your past. What did you enjoy when you were young? What were your hobbies and interests? Are there things you have always wanted to do but never felt you had the time? Try to relax in a way that is different from your work. If your job involves sitting and thinking all day, try to find leisure activities that keep you more active and involve some physical activity.

Then make up your mind that you will get involved in

recreation. It is very easy to think "I'll do it as soon as I get a chance," but when we think this way the chance never seems to come. Perhaps you need to set aside some time each week for relaxation, perhaps an evening or two or maybe a Saturday afternoon. Other people like to set a definite, realistic goal in their work and relax when they attain the goal.

When the recreation time does come, don't keep thinking about your work. I used to have a problem with this whenever my wife would suggest that we visit a shopping center. I'd feel pulled away, and all the time we were there I'd be thinking about getting back to work. One day it occurred to me that I'm losing two hours regardless of whether I relax or keep "bracing at the bit" to get home. So I changed my attitude. "Tonight we go to the shopping center," I began to think, and I learned to forget my work while we were there. The whole family has been happier since.

In all of this we must recognize the need for vacations. These should be planned by the family well in advance. Try to be realistic in your planning, so that you don't expect too much or overexert yourself. Try to do something which everyone enjoys. There are two other rules for vacations: first, don't take any work along, and second, take half the clothes and twice as much money as you think you will need!

Too Much Leisure

With the increase in technology and the resulting shorter workweek, many people are finding that they have too much leisure time. This can be as frustrating and stress-producing as overwork. It may take some creativity to find worthwhile leisure activities, but look around. What needs to be done in your home, church, or community? Can you develop some hobby in greater depth or spend some time reading to stimulate your interest and develop your mind? What can you do for others? All of this suggests activity of some sort. Such activity is much better and more fulfilling than sinking into laziness before the constantly running TV set.

Sleep

When I first joined the Navy as a young man, I reported to a training center one summer and got a rude awakening—they expected us to get up early in the morning, very early. It didn't take me long to discover the truth in the words of some sage who once remarked that "the battle of the morning is won the night before." As everyone knows from experience, it is difficult to function efficiently when we are tired.

The answer to fatigue, however, isn't always "get enough sleep," although that is a good starting place. Some people get in bed early enough but they can't seem to unwind. Counting sheep, taking hot baths, and other home remedies don't seem to help much, if at all.

The reason for this is that sleeplessness comes because we are physiologically aroused. Insomnia has a chemical basis, and that cannot be willed away when you are in bed trying to rest.

The best time to start working on the problem is during the evening, long before it is time to retire. If possible, avoid caffeine, stimulating conversation, reading that is tension-producing, intense intellectual pursuits, repetitious activity, overeating, strenuous exercise, or anything else which might get your body keyed up.

Once you get into bed you might try some of the relaxation exercises that are described in Table 3. These can relax the body and make sleep more likely. Of course noise, light, and temperature extremes should be avoided, if possible, and there is also value in focusing your mind on Scripture verses which you have committed to memory, or on something uninteresting (like the tree stump mentioned in the last chapter).

A recent study at Tufts University School of Medicine

shows that sleep can be induced by tryptophane, one of the amino acids in milk. It appears, therefore, that there is some merit in the old theory about warm milk helping us to sleep. Sex also helps. By reducing some of the tension that keeps us awake, sexual activity at bedtime can help us relax and go to sleep.

When all else fails, it may be best to stop fighting the problem. Worrying about not sleeping may churn us up and keep us awake. So it is better to read a book, listen to soothing music, or engage in some other quiet activity. Occasional use of sleeping pills also helps, of course, but with persistent use these lose their effectiveness. If insomnia still continues, it makes sense to see a physician before you start taking sleeping pills on a regular basis.

Regular Exercise: Nature's Tranquilizer

The above heading, which appeared in an alumni paper, is more than a catchy phrase. It expresses a basic truth which is often forgotten in our age of mechanical wonders. We have comfortable cars, escalators, automatic garage door openers, power mowers, snow blowers, garbage disposals, dishwashers, ovens that turn themselves off, and such a variety of other delightful labor-saving devices that we hardly have to exert ourselves at all. This can be pleasant in may respects, but it can also encourage physical laziness, and that's not good for our stress problems.

Studies have shown that when people exercise regularly they feel better, sleep more soundly, handle problems better, and are more able to cope with life. Exercise on a regular basis is good for the body, and this in turn can reduce anxiety and inoculate us so that we can better handle future stresses.

For people who enjoy sports, such activities as handball, swimming, golf, or tennis can be good stress-reducers provided they are done regularly, are not overly strenuous, and are not played with such keen competition that more stress is aroused. For others, daily jogging or calisthenics can keep us from getting too flabby or tense. Even stretching or muscle massage can be very helpful, although these should not be used as a substitute for exercise done on a regular basis.

If you are like I am, you probably find exercise boring. One way to solve this problem is to exercise to music or listen to the news during your workout. Don't do this, however, if the news of the world makes you more tense! It would be better to relax with some sound that is less realistic but more relaxing.

ATTACKING THE SOURCE OF STRESS

All of the techniques mentioned thus far in this chapter are designed to help us relax, but none really deals with the *source* of stress.

To some extent this is a futile exercise. How can one person or even a group of people tackle the way of life which engulfs us all and creates stress? The answer, of course, is that none of us can do much to alter the society, but we *can* do something about the society's influence on our own lives.

Goal-Setting

First, we can set some realistic goals. This gives direction to our lives and keeps us from drifting. It gives us a feeling of accomplishment when we reach our goals, and it helps us to be productive people. With all of this we feel more on top of things and less swayed by the uncertainties of life.

There are two kinds of goals in life—long-range and short-range.[4] The long-range goals refer to things that we want to accomplish in our lives eventually. Such goals should be general and should be made as realistic as possible (e.g., "I want to be a good teacher" is better than "I want to be awarded the 'Best Teacher in the U.S.' award").

These long-range goals can concern our careers, our businesses, our spiritual lives, or our families (e.g., "I want to raise the children to be mentally healthy, independent of their parents, and growing as Christians").

If you have never thought about personal goals, stop right now and ask yourself the following questions. How old will I be ten years from today? What will be the ages of my family members then? What would I like us all to have accomplished by that time?

Keep your long-range goals flexible so that you won't feel a sense of frustration and failure if you don't make it.

Then you should set some short-range goals that are realistic, specific, and designed to help you reach your long-range goals. Remember that you will fail at these goals sometimes. When this happens, evaluate what went wrong, reset your goal, and try again. When you achieve a goal, have a celebration. Reward yourself in some way and then push on to accomplish the next short-range goal.

Writing a Book on Stress

Three or four years ago I first decided to write this book on stress. That was my long-range goal. To accomplish this I sounded out some friends in the publishing business to see if such a book was marketable, began collecting and reading technical books on the subject,[5] taught a graduate psychology class on the topic of stress, and gave a series of lectures in three different churches. All of this was preparation to reach my goal—the completion of this book.

Then one summer I was able to block off several weeks to do the writing. My secretary scheduled no appointments, my wife and children let me go every day to a writing retreat, and I aimed toward the long-range goal of finishing the first draft of the book by the end of August.

To accomplish this goal I broke the project into short-range goals: finishing Chapter 1 by a certain date, for example, or completing Part Two by another date. Sometimes

I didn't achieve my short-range goals, and sometimes I was slowed by unforeseeable interruptions (like the visit of unexpected company). At such times I rearranged my short-term goals, worked a little harder to make up for lost time, and kept going. At times I finished a chapter earlier than anticipated, but with long- and short-range planning I was able to write these words on August 28. On the 29th I took the day off in celebration!

This goal-setting lets us experience satisfaction as we go through life and keeps us from being overwhelmed by the unexpected stresses.

The Importance of Planning

All of this implies that realistic but flexible planning can help us get things done with minimum stress. Many people plan their days each morning or at night before they retire. Budgeting your money is really planning ahead so that you don't encounter the stress of "too much month left but too little money."

The keys to proper planning are *realism* and *flexibility*. If you plan too much or are too rigid in your plans, this only leads to frustration, especially when the unavoidable arises. I once had a friend who every evening would write a list titled "Everything I Plan to Do Tomorrow." After writing the list, she told me, "I recognize that I'll only get about half of the things done." That's realistic and saves a lot of frustration.

In all of this it is helpful to write things on paper. I don't keep a diary but I do have a notebook in which I periodically jot down the pros and cons, the insecurities and anxieties, of some issue which must be planned or a problem which must be solved. When faced with a decision, I often draw a line down the middle of a page (as shown on the following page) and list my two alternatives at the top of the page. Then I fill in the positives and negatives about each alternative.

	ALTERNATIVE A	ALTERNATIVE B
Arguments in Favor		
Arguments Against		

By putting things on paper, we get a better perspective of what we are facing. Problems which have been rumbling around in our brain become more specific and manageable. You can quit worrying about missed appointments or dealines if things are written down to remind you. That is tackling some of the stresses of life at their source.

LEARNING TO BE A PEOPLE HELPER

Have you ever noticed that helping other people with their problems and stresses can have a big impact on the helper? By seeing the problems of others, our own stresses sometimes fade into insignificance. Even if this doesn't happen, helping others can show us ways for coping with stress in our own lives.

It used to be that people-helping was thought to be the exclusive domain of psychologists or other professional counselors. Now we know that this isn't true at all. In fact, there is evidence to show that friends can often do a better job at helping than can the professional.[6]

Most of us have heard the saying, "If you want friends, you must be friendly." Having a concern about other people, showing a willingness to help them even if it is inconvenient for us, being willing to listen, taking the risk of sharing our own struggles—all of this builds friendships. And one of the most effective ways to deal with stress is to share openly and communicate honestly with somebody else.

THE MIND AT PEACE

Where does stress begin? Very often it starts in the world around us, when the circumstances of life push in on us, disrupt our routines, arouse our bodies for fight-or-flight, and create both anxiety and the demand that in some way we try to cope. At other times the stresses come from within. A poor self-image, physical pain, a sense of loneliness or rejection, a negative outlook on the world—all of these are inner stresses which can be every bit as devastating (and sometimes more so) than the stresses that come from without. Regardless of the source of our stress, however, the real solutions start in our minds.

The Apostle Paul was an interesting man. After becoming a Christian his life was filled with a number of incredibly difficult stresses,[7] with which he coped very well. The reason for this, I believe, is that Paul had the right mind set. Call it positive thinking if you like, or a realistic attitude, but it began in the mind and enabled the Apostle to experience a deep and inner peace even to the end of his life, when he lived in prison under the threat of imminent death.

There are three characteristics of a mind which stays at peace regardless of the stresses of life. Such a mind knows how to deal with feelings, how to think properly, and how to initiate appropriate behavior.

Dealing with Feelings

At times Paul could have been overwhelmed with the pressures of life. He could have been angry, resentful, envious of people who weren't suffering, anxious about the future, and worried about his safety—but all of this seems to have been lacking. Surely this was because Paul had a supreme confidence in God.

"Don't worry about anything," he wrote to the Philippians. "Instead, pray about everything; tell God your needs and don't forget to thank him for his answers. If you do this you will experience God's peace, which is far more wonderful than the human mind can understand. His peace will keep your thoughts and your hearts quiet and at rest as you trust in Christ Jesus."[8] *Phl. 4:6+7*

It isn't surprising that Paul had experienced this peace in the midst of stress. Jesus had promised that it would be available to everyone, including us, if we would trust God to provide it.

"I am leaving you with a gift," Jesus had told the disciples. It is a gift of "peace of mind and heart! And the peace I give isn't fragile like the peace the world gives. So don't be troubled or afraid. . . . Let not your heart be troubled. You are trusting in God, now trust in me."[9]

Have you ever noticed how often the word "peace" appears in the headlines? We've been seeking it for years, but it doesn't seem to come. The reason for this is that true peace never comes from man's efforts alone. It only comes from God. If we don't have it, we can ask for it and expect that He will give it as He has promised.[10]

Learning to Think Clearly

Near the end of his first book, stress expert Hans Selye makes the interesting statement that the best way to deal with worry and stressful thoughts is to chase them away by concentrating on pleasant, more positive thoughts.[11] Of course this is not easy to do, but it is exactly what Paul told the pressured Philippians in a message which was mentioned earlier in this book: "Fix your thoughts on what is true and good and right. Think about things that are pure and lovely, and dwell on the fine, good things in others. Think about all you can praise God for and be glad about."[12]

Psychologists don't talk much about the mind anymore, but the Bible says plenty. Most of our problems come or are made worse because we think about things that are not pleasing to God. If we could have a thought life that was like that of Jesus, we would experience continual inner stability regardless of the stresses of life. The sure-fire prescription for peace, therefore, comes as we ask God to mold our thinking so that it conforms perfectly to His will.[13]

Notice that the Christian is not to meditate on a mantra or other meaningless symbol. We are to meditate day and night on the words of God as found in the Bible.[14] Such meditation brings a lasting peace that no advocate of TM could possibly appreciate, experience, or understand. Anxiety is accentuated when we ignore God's guidelines for inner peace and try to find our own mental routes to peace instead. Incidentally, Dr. Herbert Benson, whose work on meditation was discussed in Chapter 12, believes that prayer or religious teachings (i.e., the Word of God for the Christian) is every bit as acceptable as a mantra for bringing the relaxation response.[15] Clearly the words of Isaiah the prophet still hold: "He will keep in perfect peace all those who trust in Him, whose thoughts turn often to the Lord."[16]

Acting Appropriately

Have you ever noticed that a lot of human behavior is self-defeating? We want to succeed in life but set our goals so high that we are sure to fail. We want friends, but we make pests of ourselves so that people reject us and we are friendless.

The same thing can happen in the face of stress. In our inefficient attempts to cope we sometimes make a bad situation worse and end up with even more struggles than we had at the beginning. One of the reasons for this book is to suggest practical actions that you can take to reduce stress instead of increasing it.

The Bible gives a lot of practical advice which, if put into practice, will give us victory over stress. Of course it takes time to learn what the Bible says and to put it into practice, but Paul learned this lesson so well that he was able to rejoice, give thanks, and think positively regardless of the circumstances.[17]

It is inevitable that the forces of hell will attempt to prevent our being obedient to God. "The forces of evil are in opposition to the will of God. And the nearer a man's will approaches God's the more apparent and stronger and more formidable this opposition is seen to be. It is only when we are going in more or less the same direction as the devil that we are unconscious of any opposition at all."[18]

But Paul overcame this opposition. "I can do everything God asks me to with the help of Christ, who gives me the strength and power."[19] God still gives that help, strength, and power today, and He is the ultimate solution to the problem of stress.

EPILOGUE

Reading About Stress

One of the books in my library ends with a chapter that has the following lengthy but thought-provoking title: "Did Reading About Stress Cause You Stress?"

Perhaps you have asked yourself this same question. Sometimes when we read about stress, we are reminded of those stresses and problems in our lives which we normally keep hidden. To face these stresses, however, as you have done by reading this book, is the first step in handling and profiting from the pressures of life.

In the Biblical Book of Hebrews (12:5-11), the writer informs us that stress sometimes comes as an expression of God's love. Just as we put our children under stress to correct and discipline them, so God molds us in the same way. Such stress is not joyful at the time, but ultimately it is for our benefit, since each of us is able to profit from stress.

It is well to remember that understanding stress is helpful, acting to alleviate our stress is healthy, and trusting God in the midst of stress is healing and growth-producing. This book has been written to help you understand, act, and trust. If you can do all three you are well on your way to making the discovery that even *you* can profit from stress.

STUDY GUIDE

The preceding chapters were written for individuals to read and apply to their own lives. Often, however, a book like this can be of even greater interest and benefit if an individual thinks through some questions about the book or if a group meets together to discuss the chapters. The following questions are designed to stimulate such personal thought and group discussion, which can lead you into further self-discovery.

If you meet in a group, the members of your group should, before meeting, read the chapter to be discussed and look over the questions. As you discuss, the group leader should encourage every person to express his or her views (without forcing people to participate when they don't wish to do so), should maintain a somewhat objective perspective, should avoid talking very much, and should try to keep the discussion from getting too far off the track. For some of the questions there are no right or wrong answers, but hopefully the resulting discussion will lead you to some helpful and insightful conclusions. Please note that the following questions are merely suggestions. If you can think of questions which are better, feel free to use them. It might be more fun that way!

One final suggestion: if you meet in a group, be careful not to let the group get too large. Eight people is about ideal. More than twelve is too large if you really want to have fruitful and meaningful discussions.

CHAPTER 1: THE MEANING OF STRESS

1. What does the word "stress" suggest to you? Does it differ from tension or pressure?
2. Can you tell the difference between intense stress and prolonged stress? Can you think of some examples of each?
3. What are the major stresses of people in your neighborhood, church, and society? Do you have any of these stresses?
4. Look over the author's listing of Job's four major stresses. Can you think of modern examples of these stresses which you know about?
5. Take a few minutes to write down your own major stresses. Ask each person to look over his list, and then share one or two of these stresses with the group. Is it difficult to share like this? Is it helpful?
6. Read 2 Corinthians 11:24-28. How did Paul survive his stresses without having a psychological breakdown? Does 2 Corinthians 1:3-5 contain an answer? Do other Bible verses speak to this question of Paul's survival under stress? What do Paul's experiences and writings say about the stresses in your life?

CHAPTER 2: THE EFFECTS OF STRESS

1. What do you think of the idea that stress can contribute to the incidence of heart attacks, ulcers, or cancer? Can you think of people whose lives support or disprove these conclusions?
2. Are the effects of stress always bad? How can stress affect us in ways which contribute to our growth and development? Try to think of some specific examples of how you can profit (and have profited) from stress.
3. Take a few minutes to total up your personal LCU score by checking all items that have applied to you during the past twelve months. How should people react who have high scores?

4. What are the three stages in Selye's theory? Do you know of examples in your experience which support this classification?

5. How does stress affect you and members of your family? Does it influence you physically, psychologically, socially, and/or spiritually? Share honestly from your own experience.

6. Read Job 1:20-22; 2:9, 10; 3:1-3. How did stress affect Job? How did it affect Jonah, Paul, and Jesus? Can you learn anything from these examples to help you cope with or profit from stress?

CHAPTER 3: THE ORIGINS OF STRESS

1. "What is stressful depends on the individual," the author has written in this chapter. Can you think of things which are stressful for others but not for you? What puts *you* under stress, but not other people? How can people handle these differences?

2. What is frustration? Can you think of some frustrations that put people, including you, under stress?

3. Do you really think that change, fear, and pressure put people under stress? Do they put you under stress? Think of some specific examples.

4. Take a few minutes to jot down the causes of stress in your life. Then share some of your list with the group. Can you help each other to reduce or eliminate some of these stress causes?

5. Do you think Satan brings stress into our lives today like he did in the time of Job? If so, what can we do about this? Do the following verses help with your answer? James 1:12-15; 1 Peter 5:8-10.

6. Does God permit us to experience stress? Does He create it? If so, do we have any ideas why? See James 1:2-4; Hebrews 12:5-8,11.

CHAPTER 4: COPING WITH STRESS

1. What is emotional inoculation? In what ways can you inoculate yourselves or others emotionally?

2. In this chapter the author lists a number of common stress reactions. Which of these do you use regularly? Which do you use and wish you didn't? Can you change?

3. The chapter lists several suggestions for dealing with stress: taking inventory, building skills, making changes. Can you use any of these for meeting the stresses in your life?

4. What are some examples of "spiritual resources" which can help in times of stress? Might these resources help to prevent stress? Do you really think these resources work? Do you use them?

5. What do you think of Job's reactions to stress? Is Job a good example for coping with stress today?

6. Read Philippians 4:4-12. Does this have any message for us when we encounter stress? Notice that verses 4-7 discuss our feelings; verse 8 considers our thoughts; verses 9-12 focus on our behavior. Remember that Paul wrote these words in prison when he was doubtless under some personal stress.

CHAPTER 5: EVERYDAY STRESS

1. What are the two kinds of pressure described in this chapter? Can you think of examples of each? How do you cope with these? Can you profit from these pressures of life?

2. "We waste 80 percent of our time," the chapter states. How can we manage our time better? Are there times of the year when this becomes a special problem (e.g., vacations, Christmas, etc.)? How can we manage time pressures then?

When are you bored? How do you tackle your monotony? Do you think there are good and bad ways to deal
with boredom? What are some of each?

4. A lot of people today seem to have low self-esteem—an
"inferiority complex." Do you? Would you agree or disagree with the author's conclusion that a low view of
ourselves is "not a mark of spirituality; it is evidence of
an unbalanced theology"?

5. What is tension? How can we reduce tension? How can
we help each other reduce tension?

6. Do you think Jesus encountered everyday stress? Read
Mark 1:29-39 and notice how Jesus dealt with the pressures in His life. Does this have any practical relevance
to us?

CHAPTER 6: FAMILY STRESS

1. What are stresses facing families today? Make a list and
then put a checkmark next to the stresses that face your
family. What can be done about these stresses? Can we
profit from them?

2. Summarize what the author writes about the role of husbands and wives. Do you agree? Is this description relevant for our modern era?

3. How can we reduce parent-child conflicts? Are the
author's suggestions helpful? What would you add?

4. How can we learn to communicate better? Think of
some specific suggestions. Can you use these suggestions in your family? Can you use them in your group?
Start now.

5. Do you take your family seriously? Give examples to
support your answer. How can you take your family
more seriously? Be specific in listing things you could
do.

6. Read 1 Peter 3:1-10. How can application of these
verses help pressured families—including yours?

CHAPTER 7: SEXUAL STRESS

1. What are some of the sexual stresses that influence people in our society today? Do they affect you? Does a discussion of sex put you under stress? Be honest. Talk about the reasons some people still feel uncomfortable discussing sex. Should we feel this discomfort?

2. Make a list of the sexual temptations that influence you. Is anyone willing to share an item or two from his or her list? Do you agree that our "very character will be deeply affected by how sexuality is managed, sublimated, expressed, denied, and propagated"?

3. Do you agree that sex apart from marriage, including open homosexuality, is wrong? Does our society's widespread acceptance of these practices put Christians under unique stresses when we disagree with the society? What can be done about this conflict?

4. "The mind is our biggest sex organ and the greatest source for sexual stress." Do you agree? How can we keep our minds pure? Look again at Philippians 4:8; then at Romans 12:1, 2.

5. In the chapter, the author gives some guidelines for controlling sexual stress. Will these guidelines work? Would you add or subtract anything from the list?

6. Read Hebrews 13:4 and Ephesians 5:1-7. What is the relevance of these verses for handling and profiting from sexual stress?

CHAPTER 8: OCCUPATIONAL STRESS

1. Make a list of the five major stresses that come with your work. Share your list, or part of it, with your group. How do these stresses affect you and your family? How can you deal with them?

2. What is the meaning of each of the following: "workaholics," "the myth of indispensability," and "the fear of success"? Without naming names, can you

think of people who fit these descriptions? Do these labels apply to you? If so, what can you do about them? Seek some practical suggestions from other group members.

3. How would you define success? How does the author define success? Do you think either your definition or the author's should be changed? If so, how should they be changed?

4. How does financial stress affect people today? What are some of the stresses you and your family face over the issue of finances? Is this difficult to discuss in a group? Why?

5. According to the author, financial stress can be reduced when money is viewed realistically, managed wisely, and committed completely. Do you agree? How, in specific ways, can we meet each of these three suggestions?

6. Read 1 Timothy 6:7-11, 17-19. Are there practical guidelines here for handling occupational and financial stress? Write them down. Does Ecclesiastes 5:10 add to your conclusions?

CHAPTER 9: LIFE STRESS

1. "Most of us have encountered periods of life when we feel almost overwhelmed just with the challenge of living and doing our work." What have been the most stressful periods in your life? How did you cope? Did you profit from these times in life? In what ways?

2. Look over Table 2, "Potential Life Stresses," which appears on page 134. Where do you fit? Based on your experience and that of your friends, what would you add or subtract from this list?

3. Now look at some other parts of the table. Does this help you to understand the stresses that other people in your home, church, work setting, or community might be facing? How can you help them with their stresses?

4. In discussing senior citizens, the author gives three suggestions for facing this period of life: prepare, accept, and reevaluate. Would this be a good formula for handling the stress in other periods of life?

5. Do you know of people whose lives are "full of sound and fury, signifying nothing"? What about your life—is it really satisfying and meaningful? How could your life be more meaningful?

6. Paul wrote his Philippian letter from jail, and in Philippians 4:11-14 he expresses a struggle in his thinking. What is it? Do verses 19 and 20 give insight into the reasons for Paul's meaningful life and his desire to live on, even though his circumstances were unpleasant? Does Paul's example help people today—like you—who might be searching for more meaning in their lives?

CHAPTER 10: CRISIS STRESS

1. Have you ever been out of work? In what ways was this stressful? What is your attitude toward unemployed people? How can you help the unemployed?

2. Within recent years the divorce rate appears to have been soaring. Why is this, in your opinion? According to the author, "the best way to prevent the strain of divorce is to build a marriage which is growing instead of dying." How can this be done? Be specific and, if you are married, answer the question in terms of your own marriage.

3. How do you handle the stress of being sick? What can you learn from times of sickness?

4. Have you ever thought about your own death? What are your attitudes toward funerals, including your own? How will your survivors get along? Where will you spend eternity? Are these difficult issues to discuss in your group? Why?

5. "Grief is an emotion, a deep sense of loss which comes whenever we are cut off from contact with someone we

have loved." How have you coped with grief in the past? Are homesickness, the pain of divorce, and other separation anxieties a special form of grief? How do we profit from grief? How can we help others cope with and profit from grief?

6. Read Psalm 37:1-9. From these verses can we find some practical guidelines for handling crises? Are there other passages of Scripture which are helpful and relevant for people who are facing crises?

CHAPTER 11: RELIGIOUS STRESS

1. Does being a Christian put you under any stress? What about being a church member—does this create stress? Make a list of these religious stresses. Share them with your group. Which of these stresses come as a result of your Christianity and which come because of manmade traditions and man-centered tensions within the church?

2. How can your religious stresses be reduced or eliminated? Should they all be reduced and eliminated, or is it better to have some present?

3. What do you expect from the religious leaders in your church? Are your expectations unreasonable? Do they put the church leaders under stress? What can you do to alleviate this stress?

4. Summarize the stresses that missionaries face. Are these different from the stresses we face at home? Are missions really worth all this stress? What can *you* do about missionary stress?

5. Is your church guilty of erecting high walls to keep out hurting people? Do you welcome needy people or are you too busy to care? Be honest in your answer. What could your church do to be more concerned about stress-laden people? What could you do?

6. Read Acts 2:42-47 for a description of the early church. To what extent should this be a model for the church

today? If our churches followed New Testament guidelines for the church, what would this do to the stress in
the lives of people like you?

CHAPTER 12: ESCAPING FROM STRESS

1. Think of the people in your neighborhood. How do they
   escape from stress? How do you escape? Be honest with
   yourself and the group.
2. A speaker recently made the following statement: "In
   our society we think it is of prime importance to feel
   good. As a result we do almost anything to take away
   even the slightest bit of discomfort." Do you agree? Is it
   always necessary to "feel good"? Does this partially explain why people turn to drugs and alcohol?
3. What is your opinion of biofeedback and hypnosis? Are
   these legitimate ways for you to escape from stress?
4. How do you react to the author's analysis of Transcendental Meditation? Do you agree or disagree? Why?
   Do Psalm 1:1, 2; 19:14; 119:11-16 give any clue to
   God's truth about meditation?
5. The chapter lists several "problems with escaping."
   What are these? Are you inclined to rely on escape techniques which really might be worse than the stress that
   you want to avoid?
6. Read Proverbs 3:5, 6; Psalm 46:1, 10; Psalm 31:24; and
   Matthew 11:28-30. Are these and similar verses the
   means by which Christians escape? Is this any different
   from TM, alcoholism, or the thousands of other escape
   techniques?

CHAPTER 13: WINNING OVER STRESS

1. Think back over this chapter and this book. What are
   the main things that you have learned about stress? Are
   you now better able to cope with and profit from the
   stress in your life?

2. Look at Table 3, "Relaxation Exercises." Have you tried any of these? How did they work?

3. Look at the sections of the chapter entitled "Learning to Cope," "Sleep," and "Regular Exercise." Do you agree with the author's suggestions in these sections? Have you applied these suggestions in your own life?

4. Make a list of your life goals—long-range and short-term. Share your list with the group. How do you plan to attain these goals? What is your next step?

5. According to the author, "there are three characteristics of a mind which stays at peace regardless of the stresses of life." What are these? How do these apply to your life?

6. Read Colossians 3:2 and Romans 10:9; 5:1; 12:1, 2. Do these references provide the real solution to winning over stress? How do they apply to your life? Be specific in your answer.

SUGGESTIONS FOR FURTHER READING

The following books were helpful to the author in writing this book. An asterisk (°) indicates that the book is written by an author who openly claims to be a Christian. (P) indicates that the book is written for popular reading. The others are more technical.

Appley, Mortimer H., and Trumbull, Richard, *Psychological. Stress.* New York: Appleton-Century-Crofts, 1967.

(P) Benson, Herbert, *The Relaxation Response.* New York: William Morrow and Company, 1975.

(P) Brown, Barbara B., *New Mind, New Body: Bio-Feedback. New Directions for the Mind.* New York: Bantam Books, 1974.

°(P) Carlson, Dwight L., *Run and Not Be Weary: The Christian Answer to Fatigue.* Old Tappan, N.J.: Revell, 1974.

Dohrenwend, Barbara Snell, and Dohrenwend, Bruce P., eds. *Stressful Life Events: Their Nature and Effects.* New York: Wiley, 1974.

Gray, Jeffrey, *The Psychology of Fear and Stress.* New York: McGraw-Hill, 1971.

(P) Jacobson, Edmund, *You Must Relax.* New York: McGraw-Hill, 1934.

Janis, Irving L., *Psychological Stress: Psychoanalytic and Behavioral Studies of Surgical Patients.* New York: Wiley, 1958.

(P) Janis, Irving L., *Stress and Frustration.* New York: Harcourt Brace Jovanovich, 1969.

(P) Kiev, Ari, *A Strategy for Handling Executive Stress*. Chicago: Nelson-Hall, 1974.

°(P) LaHaye, Tim and Beverly, *The Act of Marriage*. Grand Rapids: Zondervan, 1976.

(P) Lamott, Kenneth, *Escape from Stress*. New York: Berkley Windhover Books, 1975.

(P) Levi, Lennart, *Stress: Sources, Management, and Prevention*. New York: Liveright, 1967.

Levine, Sol, and Scotch, Norman A., eds., *Social Stress*. Chicago: Aldine, 1970.

Levitt, Eugene E., *The Psychology of Anxiety*. Indianapolis: Bobbs-Merrill, 1967.

McGrath, Joseph E., ed., *Social and Psychological Factors in Stress*. New York: Holt, Rinehart and Winston, 1970.

(P) McQuade, Walter, and Aikman, Ann, *Stress: What It Is, What It Can Do to Your Health, How to Fight Back*. New York: E. P. Dutton, 1974.

Selye, Hans, *The Stress of Life*. New York: McGraw-Hill, 1956.

(P) Selye, Hans, *Stress Without Distress*. Philadelphia: Lippincott, 1974.

Torrance, E. Paul, *Constructive Behavior: Stress, Personality and Mental Health*. Belmont, California: Wadsworth, 1965.

°(P) Wagner, Maurice E., *Put it All Together: Developing Inner Security*. Grand Rapids: Zondervan, 1974.

°(P) Wagner, Maurice E., *The Sensation of Being Somebody: Building an Adequate Self-Concept*. Grand Rapids: Zondervan, 1975.

(P) Walker, C. Eugene, *Learn to Relax: 13 Ways to Reduce Tension*. Englewood Cliffs, N.J.: Prentice-Hall, 1975.

(P) Winter, Ruth, *Triumph Over Tension: 100 Ways to Relax*. New York: Grosset & Dunlap, 1976.

FOOTNOTES

CHAPTER 1

1. See, for example, M. H. Appley and R. Trumbull, *Psychological Stress* (New York: Appleton-Century-Crofts, 1967), Chapter 1, "On the Concept of Psychological Stress."
2. Hans Selye, *The Stress of Life* (New York: McGraw-Hill, 1956), p. viii.
3. Hans Selye, *Stress Without Distress* (Philadelphia: Lippincott, 1974).
4. H. S. Liddell, *Emotional Hazards in Animals and Man* (Springfield, Illinois: Charles C. Thomas, 1956).
5. Walter McQuade and Ann Aikman, *Stress: What It Is, What It Can Do to Your Health, How to Fight Back* (New York: E. P. Dutton Co., 1974), p. 6.
6. Kenneth Lamott, *Escape from Stress* (New York: Berkley Windhover Books, 1975), p. 8.
7. McQuade and Aikman, *op. cit.*, pp. 8-9.

CHAPTER 2

1. Stewart Wolf, *The Stomach* (New York: Oxford University Press, 1965).
2. Walter McQuade and Ann Aikmann, *Stress: What It Is, What It Can Do to Your Health, How to Fight Back* (New York: E. P. Dutton, 1974), p. 47.
3. "What to Do When You're Under Stress." An interview with Aaron T. Beck. *U.S. News & World Report*, September 24, 1973, pp. 48-54.
4. Quoted in Kenneth Lamott, *Escape from Stress* (New York: Berkley Windhover Books, 1975), pp. 35-6.

5. Meyer Friedman and Ray H. Rosenman, *Type A: Behavior and Your Heart* (New York: Knopf, 1974).

6. Lamott, *op. cit.*, pp. 37-8.

7. *Ibid.*, p. 39.

8. T. H. Holmes and M. Masudu, "Life Change and Illness Susceptibility," in Barbara Snell Dohrenwend and Bruce P. Dohrenwend, eds., *Stressful Life Events* (New York: Wiley, 1974), pp. 42-72.

9. T. H. Holmes, "Psychologic Screening," in *Football Injuries: Papers Presented at a Workshop* (Washington, D.C.: National Academy of Sciences, 1970), pp. 211-14.

10. Holmes and Masudu, *op. cit.*, p. 67.

11. Hans Selye, *The Stress of Life* (New York: McGraw-Hill, 1965); and Hans Selye, "Stress: It's a G.A.S.," *Psychology Today*, vol. 3, no. 4, September 1969, pp. 24-6, 56.

CHAPTER 3

1. Ronald Kotulak, "What's Behind Ulcers? Worries, Helplessness," *Chicago Tribune*, July 17, 1972. See also David Martindale, "Sweaty Palms in the Control Tower," *Psychology Today*, vol. 10, no. 9, February 1977.

2. Jerome E. Singer and David C. Glass, "Making Your World More Livable," in *Blue Print For Health*, vol. 25, no. 1, The Blue Cross Association, Chicago, 1974, pp. 59-65.

3. *Ibid.*, p. 63.

4. *Ibid.*, p. 64-5.

5. Irving L. Janis, *Stress and Frustration* (New York: Harcourt Brace Jovanovich, Inc., 1969), pp. 156-9.

6. Alvin Toffler, *Future Shock* (New York: Random House, 1970).

7. *Ibid.*, p. 20.

8. Quoted in Toffler, *ibid.*, p. 334.

9. James David Harkness, "The Toffler Future," *Human Behavior*, August 1976, pp. 16-21.

10. Walter D. Fenz and Seymour Epstein, "Stress: In the Air," *Psychology Today*, September 1969, pp. 27-8, 58-9.
11. J. Istel, "Statistical Report," *Parachutist*, 1961, vol. 3, pp. 11-12.
12. Marshall Bryant Hodge, *Your Fear of Love* (Garden City, New York: Doubleday & Company, Inc. [Dolphin Books], 1967).
13. 1 Peter 5:8.
14. 2 Corinthians 11:14.
15. Ephesians 6:10-13.
16. Job 1:9-12; 2:3-6.
17. Hebrews 12:5-11; 1 Peter 1:6, 7; James 1:1-3; 5:11.
18. Hans Selye, *Stress Without Distress* (Philadelphia: J. B. Lippincott Company, 1974).

CHAPTER 4

1. Irving L. Janis, *Psychological Stress: Psychological and Behavioral Studies of Surgical Patients* (New York: Wiley, 1958).
2. Irving L. Janis, *Stress and Frustration* (New York: Harcourt Brace Jovanovich, Inc., 1969).
3. Charlie Shedd, *The Fat Is in Your Head* (Waco, Texas: Word, 1972).
4. Matthew 11:28-30; 1 Peter 5:7.
5. Walter McQuade and Ann Aikman, *Stress: What It Is, What It Can Do to Your Health, How to Fight Back* (New York: E. P. Dutton, 1974).
6. *Ibid.*
7. "What to Do When You're Under Stress." An interview with Aaron T. Beck, *U.S. News & World Report*, September 24, 1973, pp. 48-54.
8. L. B. Murphy, "Learning How Children Cope with Problems," *Children*, July-August 1957, U.S. Department of Health, Education and Welfare.
9. E. Paul Torrance, *Constructive Behavior: Stress, Personality, and Mental Health* (Belmont, California: Wadsworth Publishing Co., 1965).

10. *Ibid.*, p. 207.
11. Quoted by Ronald Kotulak, "How to Remain on Even Keel," *Chicago Tribune*, July 20, 1972.
12. Genesis 1:27-31; Romans 3:23; 5:8; 6:23; 10:9; Ephesians 2:8, 9.
13. I Thessalonians 5:18; Ephesians 5:20.
14. Job 1:22; 2:9, 10.

CHAPTER 5

1. Dorothy Storck, "I. C. Survivors' Therapy: Let It All Come Out," *Chicago Today*, November 30, 1972.
2. Sebastion de Grazia, *Of Time, Work, and Leisure* (New York: The Twentieth Century Fund, 1962).
3. "How to Use Your Time Wisely" Interview with Alan Lakein, an authority on time management, *U.S. News & World Report*, January 19, 1976.
4. Philip G. Zimbardo, Paul A. Pilkonia. and Robert N. Norwood, "The Social Disease Called Shyness," *Psychology Today*, May 1975, pp. 69-72.
5. *Ibid.*
6. Maurice E. Wagner, *The Sensation of Being Somebody* (Grand Rapids: Zondervan, 1975).
7. Jay E. Adams, *The Christian Counselor's Manual* (Nutley, N.J.: Presbyterian and Reformed Publishing Co., 1973).
8. Daniel Goleman, "Why Your Temples Pound: Migraine and Tension Headaches," *Psychology Today*, August 1976, pp. 41-42, 76-78.
9. This quotation originally appeared in the author's article "Up from Confusion" in Denny Rydberg and Dean Merrill, *I Am Somebody: A Christian Search for Identity and Self-Acceptance* (Elgin, Illinois: David C. Cook, 1975), pp. 15-17. The next few paragraphs in this chapter are adapted from the earlier article.
10. Exodus 4:11; 6:6.
11. Jack Horn, "Love: The Most Important Ingredient in Happiness," *Psychology Today*, July 1976, pp. 101-2.

12. Psalm 75:6, 7; Jeremiah 9:23, 24.

CHAPTER 6

1. Edith Schaeffer, *What Is a Family?* (Old Tappan, New Jersey: Fleming H. Revell, 1975).
2. Lester Velie, "The War on the American Family," *Reader's Digest*, January 1973, pp. 106-110.
3. Alvin Toffler, *Future Shock* (New York: Random House, 1970).
4. E. E. Masters, "Parenthood as Crisis," *Marriage and Family Living*, vol. 19, 1957.
5. Ephesians 5:24.
6. Ephesians 5:21.
7. Larry Christenson, *The Christian Family* (Minneapolis: Bethany Fellowship, 1970), pp. 42, 44, 40.
8. Quoted by Larry Christenson, "A New Look at Christian Husbands," in Gary R. Collins, ed., *Make More of Your Marriage* (Waco, Texas: Word Books, 1976), pp. 42-3.
9. Ephesians 6:1, 2.
10. Much of the following discussion is based on Ephesians 6:1-4, Colossians 3:20, 21, and Deuteronomy 6:1-18. In this latter passage, the writer clearly ties in the idea of children's obedience to parents with parents' obedience to God.
11. Ephesians 6:4; Colossians 3:21.
12. John 13:35.
13. Hebrews 12:5, 6.
14. James C. Dobson, *Dare to Discipline* (Wheaton, Illinois: Tyndale, 1970), p. 29.
15. Mark Lee, "Reasons Marriages Fail—Communication," in Collins, *op. cit.*, pp. 65-82.
16. Charlotte H. Clinebell and Howard J. Clinebell, Jr., *The Intimate Marriage* (New York: Harper & Row, 1970), p. 93.
17. Paul Tournier, *To Understand Each Other* (Richmond, Virginia: John Knox Press, 1962).

CHAPTER 7

1. J. Rinzema, *The Sexual Revolution* (Grand Rapids: Eerdmans, 1974), p. 61.
2. *Ibid.*, p. 21.
3. William Simon, "Sex," *Psychology Today*, July 1969, pp. 23-7.
4. George F. Gilder, *Sexual Suicide* (New York: Quadrangle/The New York Times Book Co., 1973), p. 1.
5. Genesis 1:27.
6. Genesis 1:28.
7. Genesis 2:24.
8. Lewis B. Smedes, *Sex for Christians* (Grand Rapids: Eerdmans, 1976), p. 26.
9. Proverbs 5:18, 19.
10. 1 Corinthians 7:2-5.
11. Tim and Beverly LaHaye, *The Act of Marriage: The Beauty of Sexual Love* (Grand Rapids: Zondervan, 1976).
12. 1 Corinthians 6:16.
13. 1 Corinthians 6, 7.
14. 1 Corinthians 6:9, 13, 18, 19; 1 Thessalonians 4:1-8; Hebrews 13:4.
15. 1 John 1:9.
16. 1 Corinthians 10:13a.
17. 1 Corinthians 10:13b; 1 John 4:4.
18. 1 John 1:9; 5:14, 15.
19. James 5:16.
20. William Barclay, *The Gospel of Matthew*, vol. 1, rev. ed. (Philadelphia: Westminster, 1975), p. 149.
21. Romans 12:2; 1 Corinthians 2:16; Philippians 2:5, 4:8; Colossians 3:12.
22. David A. Seamands, "Sex, Inside and Outside Marriage," in Gary R. Collins, ed., *The Secrets of Our Sexuality* (Waco, Texas: Word, 1976), pp. 149-165.
23. Sex Information and Educational Council of the United States (SIECUS), *Sexuality and Man* (New York: Scribner's, 1970), p. 69.

24. Matthew 5:27, 28.
25. 1 Corinthians 6:12.
26. Smedes, *op. cit.*, p. 244.
27. This suggestion is made by Herbert J. Miles, *Sexual Happiness in Marriage* (Grand Rapids: Zondervan, 1967), p. 86. I have relied heavily on Miles' excellent book in the paragraphs which follow.
28. David Reuben, *Everything You Always Wanted to Know About Sex But Were Afraid to Ask* (New York: David McKay Co., 1969).
29. See footnote 11.
30. For a concise discussion of male and female roles, see Mary Stewart Van Leeuwan, "Femininity Today: Walking the Knife Edge," and Gary R. Collins, "Masculinity Today" in Gary R. Collins, *op. cit.*, pp. 44-68.
31. Philippians 4:8.

CHAPTER 8

1. Edgar H. Schien, "The First Job Dilemma," *Psychology Today*, March 1968, pp. 26-37.
2. Wayne E. Oates, *Confessions of a Workaholic* (Nashville: Abingdon Press, 1972).
3. Philippians 4:7, 8.
4. Romans 12:2.
5. Romans 12:6-8, 11.
6. Leon Tec, *The Fear of Success* (Pleasantville, N.Y.: Reader's Digest Press, 1976).
7. 1 Corinthians 1:31; Jeremiah 9:23, 24.
8. Philippians 4:18, 19.
9. Matthew 20:26, 27.
10. Ari Kiev, *A Strategy for Handling Executive Stress* (Chicago: Nelson-Hall, 1974), p. 11.
11. For a discussion of ways to handle anxiety, discouragement, envy, anger, etc., see the author's *Overcoming Anxiety* (Santa Ana, California: Vision House, 1973).
12. 1 Timothy 6:9, 10.

13. Matthew 6:19-34.
14. Matthew 25:15-30.
15. "Where Does All the Money Go?" Pamphlet published by Louis Neibauer Co., Inc., Jenkintown, PA 19046.
16. Malachi 3:8.

CHAPTER 9

1. J. B. Phillips, *Ring of Truth* (New York: Macmillan, 1967), p. 23.
2. Ray Cripps, "Dark Night of the Soul" (an interview with J. B. Phillips), *Guideposts*, February 1967.
3. See, for example, Gary R. Collins, *Man in Transition: The Psychology of Human Development* (Carol Stream, Illinois: Creation House, 1971).
4. Quoted in an article by Don A. Schanche, "What Happens—Emotionally and Physically—When a Man Reaches 40?" *Today's Health*, March 1973, pp. 40-43, 60-62. Much of the discussion of Levinson's research is adapted from this article.
5. Eda H. LeShan, *The Wonderful Crisis of Middle Age* (New York: David McKay, 1973), pp. 30-31.
6. Paul Tournier, *Learn to Grow Old* (New York: Harper & Row, 1972).
7. Philippians 4:5-8.
8. Quoted in Bella Stumbo, "Adding New Chapters to Your Life Script," *Mainliner*, March 1976.
9. James 4:14.
10. John 3:16; 10:7-10.
11. Philippians 1:20.
12. Proverbs 3:5, 6.

CHAPTER 10

1. D. D. Braginsky and B. M. Braginsky, "Surplus People:

Their Lost Faith in Self and System," *Psychology Today*, August 1975, pp. 68-72.

2. *Ibid.*, p. 70.

3. Louise J. Despert, *Children of Divorce* (Garden City, New York: Doubleday, 1962).

4. Mel Krantzler, *Creative Divorce: A New Opportunity for Personal Growth* (New York: M. Evans & Co., 1973).

5. Matthew 19:3-9.

6. John 4:1-30.

7. Matthew 11:28-30.

8. Irving L. Janis, *Psychological Stress* (New York: Wiley, 1958), p. 10.

9. Irving L. Janis, *Stress and Frustration* (New York: Harcourt Brace Jovanovich, Inc., 1969), p. 196.

10. L. Egbert, G. Battit, C. Welch, and M. Bartlett, "Reduction of Post-operative Pain by Encouragement and Instruction of Patients," *New England Journal of Medicine*, 1964, vol. 270, pp. 825-27.

11. Hebrews 13:5, 6.

12. Philippians 4:6, 7.

13. Joseph Bayly, *The View from a Hearse: A Christian View of Death* (Elgin, Illinois: David C. Cook, 1969), p. 15.

14. Elisabeth Kübler-Ross, *On Death and Dying* (New York: Macmillan, 1969).

15. *Op. cit.*, pp. 31-2, © David C. Cook, quoted with permission.

16. The conclusions in this section are adapted from several sources, including Fred Cutter, *Coming to Terms with Death: How to Face the Inevitable with Wisdom and Dignity* (Chicago: Nelson-Hall, 1974), and Granger E. Westberg, *Good Grief* (Philadelphia: Fortress Press, 1962). See also Melba Colgrove, Harold H. Bloomfield, and Peter McWilliams, *How to Survive the Loss of a Love* (New York: Bantam Books, 1977).

17. Hebrews 9:27.

18. Ephesians 2:8, 9.

19. Romans 10:9; John 3:15, 16; Romans 8:1.

CHAPTER 11

1. John 16:33; 14:27.
2. Albert Ellis, "The Case Against Religion," *Mensa Journal*, no. 138, September 1970.
3. Clark H. Pinnock, *Set Forth Your Case: An Examination of Christianity's Credentials* (Chicago: Moody Press, 1967), p. 85. Elsewhere, I have examined the entire religious foundation of psychology, including psychological criticisms of religion. See Gary R. Collins, *The Rebuilding of Psychology* (Wheaton, Illinois: Tyndale House, 1977).
4. For one of the most fascinating studies of ministers who left the ministry, see G. J. Jud, E. W. Mills, Jr., and G. W. Burch, *Ex-Pastors: Why Men Leave the Parish Ministry* (Philadelphia: Pilgrim Press, 1970; also E. W. Mills and John P. Koval, *Stress in the Ministry* (Washington, D.C.: Ministry Studies Board, 1971).
5. Thomas R. Teply, "What Should the Pastor Be Doing All Week?" *The Presbyterian Layman*, 1973.
6. The magazine, of course, should remain nameless. The essence of the article was later published in one of my books. See Gary R. Collins, *Man in Transition* (Carol Stream, Illinois: Creation House, 1971), pp. 174-182.
7. Peter F. Drucker, *The Effective Executive* (New York: Harper & Row, 1967).
8. This section on missionary stress first appeared under the title "Stress and the Missionary," *Trinity World Forum* (Deerfield, Illinois: Trinity Evangelical Divinity School), vol. 1, 1975.
9. Ephesians 2:13-15.
10. Howard A. Snyder, *The Problem of Wine Skins: Church Structure in a Technological Age* (Downers Grove, Illinois: InterVarsity Press, 1975), p. 21.

CHAPTER 12

1. C. William Henderson, *Awakening: Ways to Psycho-*

Spiritual Growth (Englewood Cliffs, New Jersey: Prentice-Hall, 1975).

2. Henderson's book (*op. cit.*) is the best, most concise overall summary of these and similar movements. Henderson believes that all of the movements have merit and that we should simply choose what best fits each of us. While I disagree with this conclusion, I can recommend the Henderson book to anyone who wants a brief and readable overview of what the different movements teach.

3. Clarence J. Row, "Alcoholism," in Dana L. Farnsworth and Francis J. Braceland, eds., *Psychiatry, The Clergy and Pastoral Counseling* (Collegeville, Minnesota: St. John's University Press, 1969), pp. 231-242.

4. Ruth Maxwell, *The Booze Battle: A Common Sense Approach that Works* (New York: Praeger Publishers, 1976).

5. These stages are described in detail in a number of places. See, for example, John E. Keller, *Ministering to Alcoholics* (Minneapolis: Augsburg, 1966), or Gary R. Collins, *Fractured Personalities* (Carol Stream, Illinois: Creation House, 1972), pp. 159-169.

6. Alcoholics Anonymous and Al-Anon Family groups are listed in local telephone directories. If you need more information, write AA World Services, Inc., P.O. Box 459, Grand Central Station, New York, New York 10017.

7. Ruth Maxwell, *op. cit.*

8. The most complete and fascinating introduction to biofeedback is Barbara B. Brown, *New Mind, New Body: Bio-Feedback: New Directions for the Mind* (New York: Bantam Books, 1974).

9. For example, at the University of California laboratory of psychologist J. Kamiya. See J. Kamiya, "Operant Control of the EEG Alpha Rhythm and Some of Its Reported Effects on Consciousness," in C. T. Tart, ed., *Altered States of Consciousness* (New York: Wiley, 1969).

10. See, for example, the papers dealing with hypnosis in Theodore X. Barber, *LSD, Marijuana, Yoga and Hypnosis* (Chicago: Aldine, 1970).

11. Reported in Walter McQuade and Ann Aikman, *Stress: What It Is, What It Can Do to Your Health, How to Fight Back* (New York: E. P. Dutton, 1974), p. 179.

12. Daniel Goleman, "Meditation Helps Break the Stress Spiral," *Psychology Today*, February 1976, pp. 82-86, 93.

13. In writing this article I have relied heavily on an excellent article by Pat Means, "Meditation Mania: Relaxation or Religion?" *Worldwide Challenge*, April 1976. Reprints are available free of charge by writing Worldwide Challenge, Arrowhead Springs, San Bernardino, California 92414.

14. Maharishi Mahesh Yogi, *Meditations of Maharishi Mahesh Yogi* (New York: Bantam Books, 1973), pp. 17-18.

15. *Ibid.*, p. 59.

16. *Ibid.*, p. 95.

17. Maharishi Mahesh Yogi, *On the Bagavad Gita: A New Translation and Commentary* (Baltimore: Penguin Books, 1967), p. 228.

18. David Haddon, "Transcendental Meditation Challenges the Church," *Christianity Today*, March 26, 1976, pp. 15-18.

19. See, for example, Exodus 20:3-5.

20. Herbert Benson, *The Relaxation Response* (New York: William Morrow and Co., 1975).

21. Hans Selye, *Stress Without Distress* (Philadelphia: Lippincott, 1972).

22. Colin Martindale, "What Makes Creative People Different?" *Psychology Today*, July 1975, pp. 44-50.

23. Matthew 13:15; 24:42; 1 Peter 5:8; James 4:7.

24. Matthew 6:7; cp. Psalm 1:1, 2; 19:7-14.

25. Quoted in Pat Means, *op. cit.*

26. Ephesians 2:8-10.

27. Romans 3:23; 6:23.

CHAPTER 13

1. Edmund Jacobson, *You Must Relax* (New York: McGraw-Hill, 1934).
2. This list is adapted from Winter, *Triumph over Tension: 100 Ways to Relax* (New York: Grosset & Dunlap, 1976).
3. Hans Selye, *The Stress of Life* (New York: McGraw-Hill, 1956), p. 266.
4. In writing this section I have relied on a book written by one of my former classmates, C. Eugene Walker, *Learn to Relax: Thirteen Ways to Reduce Tension* (Englewood Cliffs, New Jersey: Prentice-Hall, a Spectrum Book, 1975).
5. Some of these are listed in the "Suggestions for Further Reading" section at the end of this book.
6. This conclusion is documented and techniques for people helping are outlined more fully in the author's book: Gary R. Collins, *How to Be a People Helper* (Santa Ana, California: Vision House, 1976).
7. These are summarized by the Apostle himself in 2 Corinthians 11:24-28.
8. Philippians 4:6, 7 TLB.
9. John 14:27, 1 TLB.
10. Psalm 29:11; 119:165; Isaiah 26:3; John 16:33; Ephesians 2:14.
11. Selye, *op. cit.*, p. 268.
12. Philippians 4:8 TLB.
13. Romans 8:6; 12:1, 2; Philippians 2:5.
14. Joshua 1:8; Psalm 1:2; 19:14; 104:34; 119:12-16, 97-99, 148.
15. Herbert Benson, *The Relaxation Response* (New York: William Morrow, 1975), pp. 115-6.
16. Isaiah 26:3 TLB.
17. Philippians 4:11-13.
18. The words are those of David Bold from a book titled *Of Heaven and Hope*, quoted in J. B. Phillips, *Ring of Truth* (New York: Macmillan, 1967), p. 50.
19. Philippians 4:13 TLB.

INDEX

You Can Profit from Stress
Cassette tape album by Dr. Gary Collins

Take a positive approach to life's everyday pressures! In this series of tapes, Dr. Collins leads us through the steps to mastery over immobilizing anxiety and tension. We can not only cope with stress, but profit from it, and use its experience to benefit ourselves!
4 Tapes $19.98 4COL01

You Can Profit from Stress
Highlights of Dr. Collins' seminar on stress, given before a live audience.

Single Cassette $4.98 1COL01

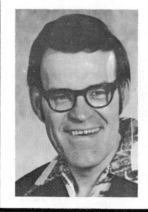

Dr. Gary Collins is Professor of Psychology and Chairman of the Division of Pastoral Psychology and Counseling at Trinity Evangelical Divinity School, Deerfield, Illinois. He has written and edited numerous outstanding books and articles on human relationships. Dr. Collins attended McMaster University, the University of Toronto, the University of London, and Purdue University, where he received his Ph.D. in Clinical Psychology. He is married and has two daughters.

How to Be a People Helper

by Dr. Gary Collins

Everyone you know has problems, and it's likely you can help them more than you realize.

Think about it! More "hurting" people are helped by friends, relatives, parents and business associates than by professional counselors. Even the counseling profession is facing this fact.

It is the objective of this book to help you be a better People Helper than you already are!
- Understand the principles of Christian discipleship—the basis of being a People Helper
- Become more sensitive to others' feelings
- Learn how to deal with "people problem" crises

Paper $3.98 DCOL02

PAK
DCOL02

BOOK
DCOL04

WORKBOOK
HCOL02

The People Helper Growthbook

by Dr. Gary Collins

A manual to accompany *How to Be a People Helper*.

■ 12 lessons to corrolate with your *How to Be a People Helper* book.

■ Each lesson includes a Bible study, personal exercises and suggested projects for a study group to do together.

■ 8½" x 11" in size, allowing for ample notetaking—will become a permanent People Helper reference in your library!

Paper $4.98 DCOL04

The People Helper Pak

For Group Study

The *People Helper Pak* includes:

■ *How to Be a People Helper* book

■ *The People Helper Growthbook*

■ *Three cassettes, conveniently packaged for easy use and storage*

■ Taped instructions to assist the group leader, plus chapter-by-chapter study of People Helper concepts

■ Bible study, home projects, group exercises—and Dr. Gary Collins' personal guidelines and suggestions for becoming *effective* People Helpers

Anyone can lead a People Helper group with this convenient and easy-to-use series of cassettes. A complete 12-lesson course in People Helping!

People Helper Pak $34.98 HCOL02 (Cassettes are not available separately.)

NEW!

SLIM GEMS

BOOK
ACOL02

CASSETTE
1COL02

Relax and Live Longer

by Dr. Gary Collins

Have you ever wanted to relax—and couldn't?
Dr. Collins packs practical, life-lengthening ideas
into this powerful Slim Gem!
- Learn how to relax.
- Eliminate the pressures that create obstacles to
relaxation.
- Discover many helpful suggestions you can put
to use every day.
48-page Pocket paperback $.98 ACOL02
See page 37 for other Slim Gem titles.

How to Be a People Leader
by Dr. Gary Collins

The nationally famous "People Helper" now tells
us about people leading—expanding your own
leadership characteristics so that you become an
example for others to develop their natural
personality resources.
Single Cassette $4.98 1COL02

11772